Karl Heinrich Koch

Mosel Wine

Newish *Fuder* casks with green chimes in the cellar of Maximin Grünhaus. These casks were made of Grünhaus oak by the retired Rudolf Biewer of Kasel on the Ruwer, who was the last cooper in the Mosel region. Coopers making big oak casks today—most often large oval casks, like *Stück* or *Doppelstück*—include Hösch, Aßmann, Mattern, Stockinger, and Sodarstvo Učakar. The best casks were often made of Slavonian oak. *Photo by Yong Truong.*

Karl Heinrich Koch

Mosel Wine

In Praise of Mosel Wine

A Translation of Karl Heinrich Koch's 1897 Tribute,
with Its Significance in His Time and Ours

Foreword by David Schildknecht

Edited by Lars Carlberg

DolmanScott

Published by Dolman Scott in 2022

First edition, revised in March 2022

In Praise of Mosel Wine

Original title: *Moselwein: Zu Lob und Preis des Moselweines*

by Karl Heinrich Koch

Translated from the German by Lars Carlberg, Kevin Goldberg, Per Linder, and David Schildknecht

Foreword by David Schildknecht

ISBN: 978-1-915351-00-5 (PoD) — ISBN: 978-1-915351-01-2 (eBook)

The moral rights of the author have been asserted.

Grateful acknowledgment is made to Edward Behr of *The Art of Eating* for permission to reprint previously published material from "Mosel Wine: Light, Zappy, and Dry" © 2016 and 2019 by Lars Carlberg

Thanks to N° elf for permission to reprint *"er zappelt."*

Cover: Vineyard terraces on Pinneberg (Pinnerkreuzberg) at Cochem by Anton Lewy.

www.dolmanscott.com

When he tasted a fresh, brisk wine, which otherwise had no faults,
he would summarize his assessment in the two words
"er zappelt."

„er zappelt."

1897

Contents

Mosel Wine

Acknowledgments

It is hard to believe that it has taken almost a decade to complete this project. Eight years ago, I remember talking to my then-girlfriend in Wiesbaden about the delays in translating Karl Heinrich Koch's *Moselwein: Zu Lob und Preis des Moselweines*. I want to thank Per Linder for taking the initial research in hand and jump-starting the work. In the process, we delved more deeply into the history of Mosel wine and made many new discoveries. David Schildknecht shared his expertise and greatly improved the translation. Kevin Goldberg provided an excellent essay on the wine trade of this period and helped with editing. I would also like to thank Wendy Ruopp, Patrick Byrne, and Stefan Schwickerath for copyediting, and especially Edward Behr for proofreading, and Yong Truong for designing the *"er zappelt"* logo and Mosel map.

We would also like to acknowledge the Datenbank der Kulturgüter in der Region Trier, whose website has been highly useful, especially all the different maps that can be superimposed on one another.

Sadly, over the last few years, a number of interested people died before they had a chance to read this book. They include relatives, friends, restaurateurs, wine writers, winemakers, wine merchants, subscribers, and acquaintances; several of them inspired me to learn more about Mosel wine.

TRIER, OCTOBER 2021
Lars Carlberg

LARS CARLBERG
MOSEL WINE

Foreword

+ —————◆——— +

Koch's Return

Since 2014, a who's who of Mosel wine estates, now numbering more than ten dozen, has participated in an ambitious annual open house that its organizers elected to call "Mythos Mosel." That name represented an odd choice. When has mythical status ever been conferred on Mosel wine? And doesn't "myth" describe precisely such popular misconceptions about Mosel wines as today's producers would want to dispel, not celebrate? The most stubborn and unfortunate of these is the one with which Lars Carlberg begins his essay on "The Heyday of Mosel Wine in the 1890s," namely that it is primarily or was "traditionally" sweet. Among the reasons for returning Karl Heinrich Koch's brief 1897 book to the public sphere is that it celebrates Mosel wine at a time when this genre was clearly almost universally dry. Another is to remind us that the 20th century is not the sole occasion when wines of the Mosel—a region whose rich historical and archeological legacy incorporates no Caesarean or Carolingian founding myth—have had to overcome degradation and disregard to gain recognition as among the world's vinous treasures.

Koch's paean to Mosel wine commences with an account of how little respect was paid it before 1880 in the German-speaking world, and a similar judgment could be leveled at nations where English is the mother tongue. Nonetheless, it surely speaks to a perception of prestige that, only three years after having occupied and departmentalized the German Left Bank of the Rhine, Napoleon deemed it important for purposes of taxation to classify Mosel vineyards. Thomas Jefferson's journals from his 1788 journey down the Rhine devote a paragraph to wines of the Mosel, passing along received opinion concerning six ostensibly superior villages—confined to the stretch between Zeltingen ("Selting") and Piesport ("Bispost"—a misspelling seemingly unique to Jefferson)—among which, he reports:

"The 1st. quality (without any comparison) is that made on the mountain of Brownberg, adjoining to the village of Dusmond." All six would figure among the eight topmost in Napoleon's 1804 ranking. A well-documented surge in plantings of Riesling during the ensuing quarter-century was accompanied by modest recognition in Anglophone markets.

Cyrus Redding's 1833 *History and Description of Modern Wines* cites an anonymous "recent" commentator as observing of Mosels: "Some of the wines have an agreeable flavour, especially the vintage [*sic*] of Brauneberg. This highly flavoured wine has within the last seven years become a fashionable beverage at the first tables in London, and when iced in summer, nothing can be more grateful." But he adds: "Although Moselle is become so fashionable, it is a cheap wine, the best Brauneberg... may be imported for three shillings a bottle into England." This at a time when Redding reports wines of the Pfalz's Mittelhaardt and Rheinhessen's Roter Hang as selling for anywhere from 8 to 18 shillings and those of the Rheingau for significantly more. Exceptionally, however, he notes the astonishingly high price that "[a] Dutch merchant is said to have paid the Abbey of Maximinus for [two casks of] a variety called Gruenhäuser, in 1793."

The 1851 edition of Redding's book—the third of five—adds to this description just three sentences apt to leave 21st-century readers shaking their heads: "[Mosel wines] are plentiful and cheap, some of them resembling the growths of France. They are sometimes sold as low as a penny the bottle in the country. The most celebrated is the Scharzberger [*sic*]." The next, 1860, edition adds considerable detail concerning the Mosel, notably in the form of what Redding describes as an "extract of a letter given verbatim from a German correspondent." Of the Mosel, this anonymous interlocutor writes:

> The wines grown on its banks are all of a lighter and less spirituous description than those from the Rhine. They are appreciated for their peculiar perfume, and are, principally during the summer, a very delicious beverage. The best Moselle wines range as follows: The Grünhäuser (a former property of the Abbey Maximin at Treves). The Feltinger [*sic*]: the best vineyards here are those of the old Schloss (Castle), the Brauneberger, Pisporter, Graacher,

Wehlener, &c. But in good vintages these wines are surpassed by the Scharzberger, and especially by the Scharzhofberger, a denomination for the hill, which was formerly a priory estate, and which produces the best of this description.

Henry Vizetelly's 1875 *Wines of the World*, based in large part on his detailed assessments "presented to both Houses of Parliament by Command of Her Majesty" concerning the wines he had tasted at the 1873 Vienna Exposition, is not only upbeat on the subject of Mosel wine, but also anticipates precisely the situation that Koch describes at the outset of his book: "The wines of the Moselle exhibited at Vienna," writes Vizetelly, "though 'innocent' enough, according to the popular German definition of them, were certainly superior to the pale, thin, feeble, and more or less acidulous growths that figure on the *karten* of German hotels under the head[ing] of 'Mosel-wein.'" Of the dozens of Mosel wines tasted on that occasion—which ranged from Winningen to Wiltingen and included two medal-winning combinations still familiar today: a Brauneberger from Richter and a Josephshöfer from Kesselstatt—Vizetelly reports that they "lack[ed] the robustness of their brethren of the Rhine, and no attempts had been made to prolong their vitality with adventitious alcohol." The results were "light and delicate, and possessed a fresh and at times even decided flavour, rendering them highly palatable." It is precisely such virtues of Mosel wines that Koch enumerates and goes so far as to suggest reflect "the individuality of the Riesling wine [in its] full, unlimited effect," wines that startled and delighted oenophiles reared on white Burgundy or "Hock," with effusive aromas, levity, zest, slight effervescence, dryness, and sheer refreshment.

"And what about today?" asked Koch before sketching the rapid late-19th-century ascendancy of Mosel wine to a level of prestige not equaled before or (thus far) since. What about today? Ironically, if Koch were to return in person, he would have missed a long low point in Mosel wine's reputation brought about not just by phylloxera, World Wars, revolutionary social upheaval, and a Great Depression—those also afflicted Germany's other growing regions and much of viticultural Europe—but also by a proliferation of sweetish mass-produced, generally non-Riesling libations labeled "Moselblümchen," "Zeller Schwarze Katz," and "Piesporter Michelsberg." In duration, global scope, and depth, the resultant slump in Mosel wine's reputation—it's nadir, a series of wine scandals in the 1980s—surely exceeded that on which Koch had looked back with little regret. But he would be returning today to a reinvigorated region and its wines that would probably by turns astonish, delight, unsettle, and befuddle him.

His greatest shock and delight would doubtless be prompted by one and the same phenomenon: today's Trier wine auctions. When Koch had written that "[t]he best wines of the Mosel have come very close to the top offerings of the Rhine in price," the record shows that he was engaging in more than a little hyperbole. But today, he could defend an even stronger claim. The auction prices being paid for young Mosel wines are on a par with those paid for any German Rieslings and eclipse those paid for wines of the Rheingau, which had set the bar in Koch's lifetime.

But what *sweet* wines! The vast majority harbor more residual sugar than Koch had probably ever confronted in a Rheingau Auslese—a circumstance unthinkable even from a technical standpoint in his day—and the stellar performers are virtually all products of an alliance between Riesling and botrytis that Koch argued takes place "undoubtedly at the expense of the [Riesling] grape's distinctive character." And what *tiny* quantities! When, in September 2014, Egon Müller's 2013 Scharzhofberger Kabinett Alte Reben achieved, by a wide margin, the record hammer price (and almost certainly the highest price ever paid, period) for a wine labeled "Kabinett"—113 euros per bottle—this was not just an exception to a decades-long nobly sweet bias, it was also the rare if not singular recent occasion when a full *Fuder*'s worth of Mosel Riesling was auctioned. Seldom do volumes of those wines specifically designated for auctioning (and nowadays typically vinified in tank, not cask) exceed the equivalent of a half *Fuder* (roughly 650 bottles); and there is often far less, from which the producer usually retains a significant share for his or her *Schatzkammer* or for later sale. In Koch's day, what passed for "trophy wines" got auctioned by the *Fuder*. Even the record auction price set in Trier by a celebrated 1893 Maximiner Grünhäuser Herrenberger represented two *Fuder* (the same volume whose sale price exactly a century earlier had struck Cyrus Redding as so remarkable), from among more than two dozen eponymous *Fuder*-size lots that this estate offered for sale on that occasion.

Apropos "Kabinett," Koch would have been amazed, but scarcely amused, at that formerly approbative term's usurpation by Germany's 1971 Wine Law, and scarcely less befuddled than most of today's oenophiles are by the whole "system" of *Prädikate*, both by these having been codified solely in terms of must weight and by the inconsistent manner in which they are now employed. (The subsequent usurpation of *"Hochgewächs"* would hardly be deemed worth bringing to our time-traveler's attention, given that this term's revival and redefinition did not persuade winegrowers or consumers for long, and it has largely fallen into disuse.)

Koch would, however, have understood and respected a legal distinction between wines from musts to which sugar had been added and those to whose musts it had not been, since reliance on the sugar in one's grapes at harvests was the touchstone of *Naturwein*. He would have found it hard to believe (as do even many of that organization's members) that today's VDP—which was until 2000 officially the *"Verband Deutscher Prädikats- und Qualitätsweingüter,"* where *"Qualitätswein"* alluded to chaptalization— permits sugaring of the must for its ostensible top category of Riesling. That is, Koch's reaction would have been disbelief even before coming to realize that, unimaginable as this would have been in his time, Mosel growers have not been compelled to harvest sugar-deficient or outright underripe grapes in at least 34 years.

We might imagine that, in principle, Koch would warmly welcome the renewed interest since the 1990s in producing dry Mosel Riesling. But today, it's not only an increasing challenge to achieve complete, complex Mosel or Saar Riesling that is dry-tasting yet innervating and alcoholically light; this also represents an ideal at odds with the zeitgeist that birthed *Grosse Gewächse*. Beginning in the late 1970s, influential proprietors in the Rheingau, Rheinhessen, the Nahe, and the Pfalz were increasingly at pains to demonstrate that "we too" can render complex dry wines "just like the French." (By no means all such advocates appeared to recognize that this would represent a *return* to dryness.) Influential German critics, gastronomes, restaurateurs, and winegrowers successfully spread word that the only good—or at least, for culinary purposes, only useful—Riesling was a legally dry, or *trocken*, one. As median must weights climbed relentlessly in response to viticultural "improvements," global warming, and fashion, dry German Riesling became increasingly full-bodied—and all the easier to sell for that.

By 2000, one heard prominent Mosel producers unabashedly expressing an intention to demonstrate that "we too" can render robust dry wines "just like those successful Pfälzer and Rheinhessen." But today, as it has dawned on even Germany's growers that bigger is not better, so in certain quarters has another realization dawned. From the right sites, with the right genetic material, and employing the right viticultural adaptations, it is possible to render dazzlingly multifaceted, lively, dry wines of well less than 12 percent alcohol. What's more, if growers of Riesling on the Mosel do not rise to that challenge, few elsewhere or with any other grape will be capable. It's past time, and not just on the Mosel, for thinking less about what "we too" and more about what "only we" can put in wine lovers' glasses. Not only would Koch applaud the championing of inimitability in Mosel wine, it's a pretty safe guess that among today's offerings, none would more delight him or imaginatively transport him back into his own time than the concentrated yet featherweight Kabinett trocken being rendered by an as yet small cadre of growers including Martin Müllen, Ulrich Stein, the Weiser-Künstler duo, and the Webers of Hofgut Falkenstein (also known as Falkensteiner Hof).

Koch would probably have as much difficulty in comprehending today's vinous buzzwords and intuiting today's conceptual framework for wine appreciation and evaluation as we have in comprehending his. We wrestle with the once ubiquitous but amorphous *"Gähre"* or the extremely broad usage of *"Gewächs"* that characterized Koch's era. (See footnotes supplied to passages in his text where these terms first appear.) He would for his part, and with no less justification, scratch his head when confronted with the likes of "terroir-driven," or for that matter with *"Gewächs,"* lately reincarnated as a Germanic equivalent to *"cru"* and the basis for what Koch referred to as "a vineyard classification according to the places of production" and dismissed as "not feasible." As for the practice, over and beyond descriptors, of "scoring" wines numerically, let alone the ubiquity that practice has assumed, it would take quite a bit of explaining; and this professional critic would not be surprised were Koch still left both scratching and shaking his head!

The time-traveler might be surprised—indeed, many of today's friends of Mosel wine are—to learn how frequently top vineyards still belong to direct descendants of those who purchased them in the course of Napoleonic secularization, their estate names now often enhanced by titles of nobility, public office, or professional credentials (though not as "professional winegrowers"!) that were subsequently bestowed by the Prussian or German Imperial governments. This means that a roster of today's landholding elite would strike Koch as familiar; though nowadays, in contrast to his era, few among them—Richter and Selbach being notable holdovers—run major parallel businesses as shippers or commissioners. And behind some names familiar to Koch now stand new owners and radical transformation. (Koch could scarcely be any more flabbergasted than today's observers at the nearly half-million-bottle production; the 100 hectares of vineyards across the entire Saar and nearby Mosel; as well as the complex network of supplier contracts that characterize Van Volxem under its ambitious 21st-century proprietor Roman Niewodniczanski.)

The greatest change in vineyard ownership and estate identity that a returning Koch would find is the widespread appearance on labels of family names other than those of huge landowners or nobility. This is a change that anyone born before 1970 has witnessed in his or her lifetime: the rise of the small-scale grower with middle-class means not just as vinifier and bottler but sometimes as qualitative standard-bearer for a village or even an entire region. Peruse Frank Schoonmaker's 1956 classic *Wines of Germany*, or Mosel-veteran O.W. Loeb's 1972 *Moselle*. You will find the Haags of Braunberg mentioned in the former, though not, surprisingly, the latter. You will search in vain for the names Haart, Merkelbach, or Schaefer—all families who were bottling impressive wines by the 1960s. Nor will you find a single Christoffel or Clüsserath, despite multiple options. That's not to mention the many talented Mosel natives and outsiders who since the 1980s have become winegrowers not due to any family association, but solely out of passion for this region's Riesling. The prestigious proprietor who personally engages in those vineyard labors whose rigors Koch extolled, and who personally calls the shots at every step of vinification, élevage, and marketing? That is a novelty of our time, and one that has immensely enriched the region Koch so cherished.

Our imaginary time-traveler could not but be delighted with this late-20th- and early-21st-century enrichment, because the Mosel's human resources, along with its landscapes, are the subjects—after Mosel Riesling itself—about which he most rhapsodized. The landscapes and major vineyards would still be recognizable to him, though shrinkage of the Mosel's overall vineyard surface—despite a significant recent uptick in the recultivation of abandoned sites—would be strikingly evident, especially on the Lower Mosel; and obvious neglect or in certain instances outright abandonment of once important sites would distress him, as it should us. He would doubtless remark on the wholesale replanting of the prestigious Geisberg (adjacent to today's Ockfener Bockstein), then be shocked to learn that just eight years ago it was overrun by four decades' worth of undergrowth and legions of young trees.

Koch would recognize some familiar patches along Mosel and Saar still planted in *Einzelpfahlerziehung*, their vines labor-intensively trained to single wooden stakes occasionally even (as in his day) with willow and straw. Among the dwindling number of *Moselaner* who perpetuate the art of binding vines in this manner, nearly all of them—just as in Koch's time—women, are some whose grandparents he could conceivably have met. But Koch would not be entirely shocked by the wire-trained regimentation that nowadays dominates even the Mosel's steep slopes. The Pfalz introduced that innovation in the 1840s, and by Koch's time it had made significant inroads into Austrian Baden, the Rheingau, and Rheinhessen, whence the name "Oppenheimer Drahtanlage" under which it was introduced to the Mosel sometime around 1880. In 1909, following smaller experiments deemed successful, the Prussian State would employ wire training on a portion of its new model estate Domäne Serrig. It would hearten if not amaze him to discover how many Mosel vines are still-productive veterans of his own time.

Koch would immediately grasp the vital importance of protecting and restoring the Mosel's vineyard landscape as well as its heritage vines. While he would not recognize the rubric "genetic," he would realize that old stands of vines comprise a repository of ancient wisdom in *sélection massale* as pursued routinely until the early 20th century but largely abandoned with the advent of clones. And a widespread, conscious return to "old ways" in many Mosel vineyards and cellars—encompassing newfound demand for classic *Fuder* casks and basket presses—would cheer and amuse him. On balance, it seems unlikely that Karl Heinrich Koch would be any less inspired by the 21st-century Mosel than he was by that of the 1890s. And much of what inspired him then, as you will read, are the things that inspire us about the Mosel and its Rieslings today. Hopefully, in light of the intervening, often tumultuous 124 years, we are that much more acutely aware not to take those things for granted.

CINCINNATI, OCTOBER 2021
David Schildknecht

Introduction

In 2010, Lars Carlberg discovered Karl Heinrich Koch's *Moselwein* at the Weberbach city library/archive in Trier while doing research for the former exporting business Mosel Wine Merchant. The original was published in paperback, and the library has two copies. Lars suggested that one of them needed to be refurbished, which was done as a hardcover by a local bookbinder. (A decade later, the other copy's binding is still taped together and needs to be repaired. Both copies have an extra page at the front of the book with the name of the Trier wine estate owner and merchant Bruno Rendenbach, whereas another copy found online has the name of the Traben-Trarbach wine estate owner and merchant J.W. Huesgen at the bottom of the front cover.) Lars quickly became fond of the book, purchased his own original copy at an antiquarian bookshop in Wiesbaden, and gradually started to think about a translation into English. At an early stage, Lars involved his friend Yong Truong in that plan. Yong measured the book and took photos of it for our project. Lars also approached a couple of book publishers about doing a translation in 2011.

Almost two years after his discovery, Lars launched larscarlberg.com, while I was between jobs, which gave me time to visit different wine estates in the Mosel Valley with him. On one of those trips, Lars shared his enthusiasm for Koch's book on Mosel wine and asked me if I would be interested in helping him.

During the summer of 2012, Lars and I transcribed the book from a copy published on dilibri (a digitalized collection of the State of Rheinland-Pfalz), which has been a useful resource. Besides the book, we have had access via dilibri to certain old wine periodicals, books, lists, and maps. Once we had finished a rough translation in September 2012, we asked David Schildknecht if he would be keen to write a foreword. He said yes and also offered to help with the translation, which still needed a lot of work. Later on, Patrick Byrne and Kevin Goldberg edited our translation, before David put the finishing touches on it.

When we started our project, there was very little information on Karl Heinrich Koch in the sources available to us online or in Trier and Luxembourg. I had an inkling that we might find something in the archives of the city of Mainz, and in the spring of 2014, I suggested to Lars that we take the train there. We spent two fruitful days in the archives, where I found not only Koch's biographical data but also his home addresses in Mainz. We strolled through the city and visited all of them.

After that trip, we returned to Trier's city library, which has the late-19th- and early-20th-century Mainz weekly magazine *Weinbau und Weinhandel* and the Trier weekly *Der Winzer*. In one issue of *Weinbau und Weinhandel*, we found the first ad for Koch's *Moselwein*. Thanks to this ad, we knew that the book had been published in the summer of 1897; the date was not in the book and had been forgotten. I also corresponded with the city archives in Koch's native Herford, and the staff there was helpful in giving me information about his family and early life.

An advertisement for the original book. *Photo by Anja Runkel, courtesy of Stadtbibliothek/Stadtarchiv Trier.*

In late August of 2021, Lars discovered an original copy of *Moselwein* with a handwritten note by Koch himself. He suggested that I should buy it, which I did. The note on the title page confirms what I understood all along that Koch worked alongside a barrel-maker in Mainz. His name was Stephan Horberth, who coined the phrase *"er zappelt."*

We have made a few adaptations to the original text—namely, we have switched to the current place and site names and have converted the obsolete measurement *Morgen* to hectares. Further, we have added numerous notes to improve the readability and clarity of the text. We also chose to abbreviate the following metric units: kilometer (km), hectare (ha), and hectoliters per hectare (hl/ha).

A few words on prices mentioned in the book:

Gold standard

When *Moselwein* was published in 1897, Germany and many other countries based their monetary systems on the gold standard—i.e., they used gold as the official reserve asset. This implied fixed foreign exchange rates: one had to pay 4.19 marks to the dollar and 20.43 marks to the pound sterling. This historical mark is often referred to as the *Goldmark*.

Prices of publications

Koch's book *Moselwein* cost 1 mark and his book *Die Mittelrheinischen Handelsweine* cost 2 marks. A yearly subscription to the twice-weekly periodical *Deutsche Wein-Zeitung* was 15 marks and the weekly illustrated magazine *Über Land und Meer* 14 marks.

Salaries

The Alsatian delegate to the 1898 Wine Congress in Trier reported that a vineyard worker in Ockfen on the Saar earned a daily wage of 2 marks. With a six-day workweek that would mean 52 marks a month, which was in line with the prevailing wage for unionized workers of 48 marks per month.

A teacher at a public school earned a monthly salary of 104 marks; the headmaster was paid 137.50 marks.

Prices of wine

If we use as a reference Reichsgraf von Kesselstatt's lowest price for a *Fuder* cask of Piesporter, an example cited by Koch, the amount was 3.35 marks per liter, which could buy 14 liters of beer or almost 9 liters of milk. (A half-liter of beer was 0.12 marks and a liter of milk was 0.19 marks.) The vineyard worker in Ockfen would have had to put in almost two days of work! These wines were indeed luxury goods.

In his book *Mittelrheinische Handelsweine*, published in 1893, Koch introduced a system of rating wines, from very fine to lesser, based on the prices paid for a *Stück*, an oval 1,200-liter cask used in the mid-Rhine regions. A conversion to the traditional Mosel *Fuder* cask, assuming 975 liters, gives us the following table:

	Range in marks	
	from	to
Very Fine Wines	2439	...
Fine Wines	1625	2438
Medium Fine Wines	1219	1624
Medium Wines II	813	1218
Medium Wines I	609	812
Lesser Medium Wines	407	608
Lesser Wines		406

At the beginning of Koch's book, he refers to the 1895 auctions in Trier that were held in two weekly sessions in March. These spring wine auctions were well attended—the Trier semimonthly wine magazine *Weinmarkt* notes that there were visitors from England, Belgium, and the Netherlands. Further, many well-known German wine merchants who had never been to Trier before were also in attendance, which was another indication that the golden age of German wine was in full bloom (for more on this, see Kevin Goldberg's essay).

At the 1895 auctions, von Kesselstatt's most expensive *Fuder* of 1893 Piesporter, at 9,060 marks, was actually second in price to a *Fuder* of 1893

Maximiner Grünhäuser Herrenberger (the present-day Abtsberg vineyard), which fetched 9,440 marks. Third was a *Fuder* of 1893 Scharzhofberger from the Hohe Domkirche at 7,970 marks. If we look at the average prices paid per *Fuder* of the 1893 vintage at these auctions, von Kesselstatt had the highest prices (Piesporter), followed by Bischöfliches Priesterseminar (Erdener Treppchen), Hohe Domkirche (Scharzhofberger), and Erben Wwe. Rheinart from Saarburg (Geisberger and Bocksteiner). At the 1896 auctions, as Koch notes, even higher prices were paid for the 1893 vintage.

As recorded in the *Deutsche Wein-Zeitung* between April and June 1895, the 1893 vintage of Rhine wines, at auctions in its regions, fetched much higher prices than the 1893 Mosel wines did in Trier. In the Pfalz, 1,000 liters of Ruppertsberger Reiterspfad from Georg Siben Erben sold for 12,030 marks; in the Rheingau, the Schloss Johannisberger (converted to a *Fuder* of 975 liters) went for 19,516 marks and the Steinberger for a whopping 26,813 marks! In other words, the 1893 Steinberger commanded almost triple the price of the 1893 Grünhäuser. So there is no evidence for Koch's claim in the book that the prices paid for the best Mosel wines approached those paid for top Rhine wines.

Per Linder

Mosel Wine

What scent is that I catch?
What so exudes the breath of May
And spices the very air?
Unveil for me the spray of flowers.
    Hey, hurrah!
A Mosel sparkles in the glass.
Upon my word, hurrah,
None other could it be.
             Gustav Pfarrius

Waiter, a bottle of *Kutscher*! The *Kutscher* arrives and on the bottle flashes the label "Piesporter." That's how it was as recently as thirty years ago all over northern Germany, where heaven knows what jokester bequeathed to the lowliest, cheapest wine served in inns and bars the honorific *"Kutscher."*[1] And more or less everyone knew that the *"Kutscher"* had its origins in Piesport. Mosel wine was written off as a fad, which, as such, naturally wouldn't take a big bite out of one's wallet, and Piesport—now Piesport is such a beautiful and special name, so it is understandable why it was bound to outstrip in fame all other Mosel wine names.

---

1. Literally, "coachman." *Kutscher* was an old Rheingau term for plonk. The idea was that wine served at an inn to a coachman or servant was the cheapest drink.

7

That's how it was thirty years ago! And what about today? At the Trier spring wine auction[2] held in 1895, the 1893 Piesporter wines from Graf von Kesselstatt[3]—a total of thirty-eight *Fuder*[4]—were sold at 3,270—4,040—5,000—6,040—7,070—9,060 marks for a *Fuder* of 975 liters, so the lowest quality *Fuder* was auctioned at 3,270 marks (equal to about 3.35 marks per liter) and the best *Fuder* at 9,060 marks (equal to about 9.30 marks per liter).

Yet another reminiscence: In the sixties, I personally witnessed in Mainz, the center of the mid-Rhine wine trade, how lesser, cheaper wines from the Mosel arrived in shiploads, not to be shipped from here around the world as Mosel wines, but, rather, to be blended with Rhine wines. On the Mosel, one paid less than on the Rhine, so one could more cheaply supply Mosel wine as "Rhine wine." But these times are long gone. At the moment, not a single drop of Mosel wine comes to Mainz for that purpose. But the attentive observer sometimes finds evidence today that

2. The Trier wine auctions were held in March and April at the Viehmarkt—the primary auctions at the Katholische Bürgerverein and some secondary ones at the Bavariahalle. (Mosel wines had also been auctioned in Mainz as early as the late 1870s.)

3. Technically, Count Kesselstatt was "Reichsgraf von Kesselstatt," a title conferred on his family in 1776 by the Holy Roman Emperor Josef II; in the 1890s, it was adopted as the official name of the estate, which it still is. (The full official name was Reichsgräflich von Kesselstatt'sches Majorat zu Trier.) Between 1854 and 1893, the imperial count acquired four former monastic properties: in Graach (Josephshof), Piesport, Kasel, and Oberemmel. The estate's vineyards in Piesport included various top sites, including Goldtröpfchen and Falkenberg. (For more on old site names, see glossary.) The 1898 Wine Congress in Trier highlighted the family's impressive holdings on the Saar (formerly owned by Mohr in Oberemmel), announcing that its "[g]reat sites include: Agritiusberg, Euchariusberg, Herrenberg, Karlskopf, Raul, Rosenberg, Scharzberg, Scharzhofberg, Wiltinger, Zuckerberg." The main cellar, with a capacity of 500 *Fuder*, was at Palais Kesselstatt in the Liebfrauenstraße 9 in Trier, where some wines were estate-bottled as early as 1893 with "Gräflich von Kesselstatt'sche Verwaltung" branded on the corks.

4. A cask, holding roughly 1,000 liters, traditionally used for fermenting and maturing Mosel wine (also called a *Moselfuder*); a half-sized cask, or *Halbfuder*, held roughly 500 liters. The oval casks, such as the 600-liter *Halbstück* or 1,200-liter *Stück*, were traditionally used in the Mittelrhein, Nahe, Rheinhessen, and Rheingau, though use of *Fuder* is occasionally recorded in the Mittelrhein. In the boom years of the 1890s, the standard-size *Fuderfass*, or *Fuder* cask, was either 960 (predominant in the Mittelmosel) or 975 liters. In 1889, the Mosel and Saar growers' association failed to agree on a standard size of 1,000 liters. Mosel wine was both raised in and sold by the *Fuder*. At the Trier wine auctions, whoever successfully bid on a numbered *Fuder* was responsible for picking up the wine within eight weeks of the purchase date and, in most cases, received the wine in cask. A producer's best wine of a given vintage was sometimes listed as "*bestes Fuder*." See frontispiece.

Mosel-like *Kreszenzen*[5] are sought after in other German winegrowing
regions—that's how great is the competitive pressure for Mosel wine
whose distinct characteristics have made it the public's darling.

Mosel wines have become so fashionable that in the middle of Rhine
wine country they are in direct competition with the local product. Who
would have thought such a thing possible? That the wine bars in Mainz
would serve racy Mosel wine by the glass, in the very city where only the
rich, soft wines of Rheinhessen's hinterland used to be served like that![6]

What explains the popularity of Mosel wine? Could it have emerged
so overwhelmingly if it were only a mere fad?

Formerly, the public made short work of judging Mosel wines, which
were constantly being compared to Rhine wines.[7] Rhine wine is sweet;
Mosel wine is sour: that was an unshakable axiom. This basic rule—almost
brilliant in its simplicity—was often enough the determining factor when
it came to deciding between Mosel and Rhine wines.

But one has gradually discovered that Mosel wine possesses characteristics
other than just acidity. One has learned to understand it. What does it have
and what does it not have? Even the traits that are absent play an important
role when rating wine; it is not only the positive traits that are relevant.
The expert has a whole arsenal of descriptors for both, which, admittedly,
might sound cryptic to the outsider. But, in the case of Mosel wine, one

5. *Kreszenz* (or *Krescenz* or *Creszenz* or *Crescenz*), like *Wachstum* (literally, "growth"), once
routinely appeared on labels and lists in conjunction with a producer's name as a sign that the
wine had been made from estate grapes. A further implication was that the wine had not been
chaptalized. The term *eigenes Gewächs* was also regularly applied to a wine from a proprietor's
own vineyards. The now-ubiquitous word *Weingut* rarely appeared on a wine label or list. Koch's
point is that customers were beginning to prefer wines labeled with the name of the producer.

6. Except for the Roter Hang, or "Red Slope," and a few other places on the Rheinfront,
Rheinhessen was known mostly for quantity; Koch's word "hinterland" alludes, in large part,
to the Hügelland, or "hill country," which includes gentle slopes and fairly flat terrain in the
southern area of Wonnegau, then planted more to Silvaner than Riesling. Mosel wines were
said to be similar to young Rheinhessen wines. The Rheingau also offered light, brisk wines,
but was best known for richer higher-end Auslesen.

7. "Rhine wines" meant, for the most part, wines from the Rheingau, Rheinhessen, and the
Pfalz, but also the Mittelrhein and the Nahe (which only became an official wine region with
the 1971 Wine Law). During Koch's time, merchants often sold Nahe wines as Rheinhessen or
Mosel wines. Heinrich Puricelli of Schloss Kautzenberger and Rudolf Anheuser were a couple
of notable exceptions, auctioning their estate wines by the *Stück* or *Halbstück* at the Hotel Adler
in the spa town of Kreuznach (known after 1969 as Bad Kreuznach).

can specify a number of commonly understood positive and negative qualities, and I cannot resist the temptation to line them up against one another in order to explain the general characteristics of Mosel wine. It might be best to start with the missing traits.

> Mosel wine is not heavy, big, and full;
>> it isn't leaden, lush, fat, and schmaltzy;
>> it isn't plump and opulent;
>> it isn't soft and bland;
>> it isn't dull and aloof;
>> it isn't languid and lifeless;
>> it isn't spirituous;
>> it isn't deeply colored;[8]
>> it isn't, finally, dainty and sweetish, nor is it sweet, even if it is often described that way.

> But Mosel wine is light and fleeting;
>> it's delicately sparkling, gossamer, floral, spicy, and piquant;
>> it's elegant and gulpable;
>> it's firm and steely;
>> it's racy and full of character;
>> it's full of life, crisp, and slightly effervescent;
>> it's lightly colored, glimmering green-golden.

For many years, I worked with a Rhenish master cooper,[9] who was blessed with a fine nose and palate for wine. When he tasted a fresh, brisk wine, which otherwise had no faults, he would summarize his assessment in the two words *"er zappelt."*[10] This was the highest praise that he would

8. In contrast to the dominant practice in the Rheingau, growers in the Mosel tried to pick the late-ripening Riesling grapes at full ripeness but *before* botrytis set in, and they pressed the grapes on the same day, to keep the freshness, liveliness, and green color—the so-called Mosel green.

9. The coopers, or barrel-makers, who were in practically every village (none remain on the Mosel today), even assisted the estate owners and wine merchants at auctions, such as the master cooper Gelhausen for the head forester Geltz's Saarburger (Rausch), Bocksteiner, and Geisberger wines, or master cooper Feilen for Frau Wwe. Amlinger-Keller's Bocksteiner (Zickelgarten) and Neuwieser wines. (Nik Weis now owns Zickelgarten and Neuwies, plus other vineyards in Bockstein.) By the 1890s, it was standard practice that auction wines could be tasted from cask three days before the event, or from sample bottles—identified by village or vineyard, vintage, and cask number—before and during the auction.

10. Koch's delightful play on words is not fully captured by the English adjective "zappy." The German verb *zappeln* primarily means "to wriggle" or "to fidget," evoking the animation conveyed by Mosel Riesling's typical bright acidity and *Spritz* from dissolved CO_2. But *zappeln lassen*, literally

give. The same can generally be said of Mosel wine: "It awakens the senses." And it unfolds the whole splendor of its aroma and bouquet. But who can describe aroma and bouquet? To do so would be roughly the same as to convey to a blind person what the color blue means. And yet, in the case of Mosel wine, there are certain words that can describe these fleeting virtues it possesses. The character of the grape is expressed in the aroma and bouquet of Mosel wine more than in any other wine, and that is what is so appealing about this juice of the vine, not only for the expert but for everyone. The Mosel grows firm-skinned grape varieties,[11] among them the excellent Riesling, this wonderful German grape variety, of which no nobler can be found anywhere in the world. To a large extent, this is really Mosel wine's hallmark, the one feature that distinguishes it from other wines—a characteristic given to it consistently and specifically by the stiff-skinned varieties grown on slate soil because it has not been weakened by the addition of blander juice from soft varieties.

It is well known that on the Rhine—and particularly in the Rheingau, but occasionally also in other places[12]—wines are produced entirely from pure Riesling, and that this is what most of all gives Rhine wines their old, well-deserved reputation. But we also know that the Rheingau is the classical region for the production of fine wines from the so-called

"leaving one to fidget," is a common expression for leaving a person in suspense or on tenterhooks in anticipation of something, a nice allusion to the intrigue that the best Mosel Rieslings deliver on first whiff and sip. In Heinrich Hoffmann's 1845 children's book *Der Struwwelpeter* ("shock-headed" Peter), Zappel-Philipp (Fidgety Philipp) was the hyperactive young boy who could not sit still at the table. In the 19th century, *zappeln* described a fluttering heart, something Mosel Riesling is also known to on occasion engender! Use of this brilliant metaphor in connection with wine may well be unique to Koch's barrel-making colleague, whose name was Stephan Horberth and who was born in Gaulsheim, a district of Bingen, in 1849.

11. Riesling was considered more frost-hardy and rot-resistant, thus later-ripening than the so-called soft grape varieties.

12. The other places best known for Riesling at the time were the Pfalz's Mittelhaardt, especially the top sites in Forst (Kirchenstück, Jesuitengarten, Ungeheuer), and the Rheinhessen's Rheinfront—in particular, the Roter Hang at Nierstein and Nackenheim. The prominent Heinr. Schlamp jr. estate (today's Schätzel) annually auctioned in Mainz his Rieslings, including Spätlesen and Auslesen. Each *Stück* or *Halbstück* held wine from a specific site in Nierstein, such as Pettenthal, Hipping, Fuchsloch (now a part of the enlarged *Einzellage* Niersteiner Hipping, along with other former sites, such as Flächenhahl), or Rehbach (a large part of the post-1971 *Einzellage* Niersteiner Pettenthal). Announcements from Schlamp included detailed, site-specific descriptions of each offering. In 1890, Carl Gunderloch, a banker in Mainz, acquired the former Simmler'sches Gut in Nackenheim, and auctioned his Nackenheimer wines, also Auslesen, by the *Stück* and *Halbstück*.

botrytis-affected Riesling grapes, and no matter how incomparable the *Hochgewächse*[13] of good years are, the vinification of botrytised grapes is undoubtedly at the expense of the grape's distinctive character. Other highly valuable characteristics are achieved, but the actual Riesling character is lost.

It is a peculiarity of production on the Mosel, however, that special care is taken to bring the individuality of the Riesling wine to full, unlimited effect, and its success can be seen in the prices recently paid for the *Hochgewächse* of the Mosel. The best wines of the Mosel have come very close to the top offerings of the Rhine in price, but not in style. Mosel remains Mosel. The charm is to be sought in the unfolding of what makes Mosel wine unique, which is what has gradually won the public's favor.

There is only one Mosel wine. Despite the range of quality and price for Mosel wine (a *Fuder* may sell for anywhere between 400 and 12,750 marks!), there are traits that are present in all examples. The apple does not fall far from the tree. Even the lesser wines show clearly that they come from Mosel grapes, and many a *Fuder* among them has attributes that give an idea of the glorious splendor that the Mosel's best *Gewächse*[14] can engender. Mosel wines include those grown immediately downstream from Trier and also those from the lower reaches of the Saar—more on this later.

A classification according to the places of production is not feasible. Not all that grows in the vineyards of Piesport, on the great Brauneberg hillside, or in Oberemmel, etc. is top quality. One could rank the individual vineyard sites on the basis of the property tax assessment, which has introduced a classification in eight brackets,[15] but this would require an

13. Formerly, *Hochgewächs*, which literally means "exalted growth," referred to an ostensibly top wine, usually an Auslese. In the Rheingau, *Cabinet* was long used to designate the finest reserve wines, sometimes Auslesen, such as the famous and expensive Schloss Johannisberger and Steinberger. By the 1920s, *Hochgewächs* mainly referred to Auslesen, Beerenauslesen, and Trockenbeerenauslesen. (The word *Gewächs* itself enjoyed very broad meaning.)

14. See note 5 on *Kreszenz*.

15. Koch refers to the property tax assessments in Franz Josef Clotten's 1868 *Saar und Mosel Weinbau-Karte* (Viticultural Map of the Saar and Mosel) for the district of Trier. See pages 90–93. The map, which was a vineyard classification used for marketing Saar and Mosel wines, listed most of the top sites and simplified the eight Prussian tax brackets to three: 1 and 2 were signified by dark red; 3, 4, and 5 by light red (or light brown on the 1890/1906 editions); 6, 7, and 8 by beige. The tax assessments were based on the net income on a *Fuder* sold between 1816 and 1832. They were the work of a Prussian bureaucrat from Frankfurt an der Oder, Otto Beck, who was based in Trier. The first of four editions of Clotten's map was printed in 1868 (500 copies);

enormous amount of work and would not result in a useful overview. The following general statements, however, are possible.

The best growths[16] come from Scharzhofberg, Bockstein, and Geisberg, from Agritiusberg, Rosenberg, and the site of Raul on the Saar; Piesport, Braunenberg, Bernkastel (Doctor), Josephshof, and Zeltinger Schlossberg[17] on the Mosel. Since the remarkable results of the 1893 vintage, Maximiner Grünhäuser Herrenberger[18] from the Ruwer also belongs in this category.

This is followed by other growths traveling downstream by location: a) on the Saar: Ayler, Scharzberger,[19] Kanzemer, Wawerner Herrenberger; b) on the Mosel: Thiergärtner, Avelsbacher, Augenscheiner, Kaseler, Mertesdorfer, Karthäuserhofberger (the last three in the Ruwer Valley),

the last, from 1906, shows extensive new plantings, especially on the Saar and Ruwer (for more on this, see Lars Carlberg's essay). The Prussians also made similar color-coded tax maps of the Lower Mosel (1897/1908), Nahe (1900/1901), and Middle Rhine (1902/1904). Heinrich Wilhelm Dahlen—who as managing editor of *Weinbau u. Weinhandel* reviewed Koch's *Moselwein* in the August 14, 1897 issue—published a separate tax map of the Rheingau (1885), but he was not the first author to classify and map the region's vineyards (see note 107).

16. *Gewächs*, or "growth," in Koch's day, did not imply the notion now fashionable among members of Germany's VDP association that "the narrower the geographical scope, the higher the [implied] wine quality." Rather, *Gewächs*, though it sometimes referred to a vineyard (e.g., Dhroner Hofberg), most often referred to a village's prime slate slopes collectively. And village is how most Mosel Rieslings of the era were identified at auction. Rarely did vineyard designations, where employed, correspond closely to the surface areas of today's *Einzellagen*, the official "single sites" delimited by Germany's 1971 Wine Law. (That lack of correspondence is detailed in some of the footnotes that follow.) Since 2014, Mosel growers have also been permitted to register and use on labels the names of so-called *Gewanne*, or place names (*lieux-dits*), as enshrined on the cadastral map. Sometimes these are revived names that had disappeared from labels after 1971 but were associated in Koch's era with high-quality wine. The name of a registered *Gewann* can appear on a label either with or without mention of its *Einzellage*, though the latter option lapses with vintage 2021. Any designation of *Einzellage* or *Gewann* must be accompanied on a label by the name of its village, even if the official label with the village name is treated as a "back label."

17. The renowned Schlossberg ("castle hill") vineyard in Koch's time was the area around the ruins of the castle, or *Burg* (also the place name of this location), within the present *Einzellage* Zeltinger Sonnenuhr.

18. Maximiner Grünhäuser Herrenberg matches what was later designated as Maximin Grünhäuser Abtsberg, hence the inscription "Maximiner-Grünhäuser-Herrenberg" on the 1873 stone gate at the foot of that slope. The von Stumm Halbergs' 11-ha holding, which included Bruderberg, had two variant spellings: "Maximin Grünhäuser" or (more commonly) "Maximiner Grünhäuser."

19. See note 58.

Neumagener, Dhroner, Minheimer, Ohligsberger, Neuberger,[20] Geierslayer,[21] Paulinsberger, Elisenberger, Niederberger, Graacher, Wehlener, Zeltinger, Ürziger, Erdener, Lösenicher, Kinheimer, Trarbacher, Trabener, Enkircher.

Then come the remaining wines of the Middle Mosel and those of the Lower Mosel, among which Cochem, Kobern, and Winningen distinguish themselves with better-quality production.

The fact that Mosel wines have only in recent times gained in recognition and reputation probably has to do with the poor access to the region. Until the second half of this century, the Mosel Valley was dependent on waterways for its trade with the rest of the world. Only then was the Mosel road constructed, initially from Koblenz to Alf, and later, to Zell, Trarbach, and Bernkastel. In 1879, the Mosel railway route between Trier and Koblenz came into operation, and it is only from that point on that the region can be regarded as really accessible.[22]

A small but active wine trade developed on the Mosel, adapting to the new situation, and it quickly found a way to market Mosel wines with unprecedented success. It was mainly with the lower- and mid-range qualities that fresh ground was broken with consumers. Production managed to keep pace. The whole world observed with astonishment the results of the well-organized Trier wine auctions in 1895, 1896, and 1897. Nowadays, lesser-quality wines are able to bask in the glory of the fine Mosel wines, and so, today, there is a lovely reciprocity. The ordinary wines help the fine

20. The Neuberg ("new hill") vineyard is today the *Einzellage* Wintricher Geierslay.

21. "Geierslay" ("vulture's slate") as a vineyard area probably included portions of today's *Einzellagen* Wintricher Ohligsberg and Wintricher Großer Herrgott. ("Geierslayer" had various spellings and was used on occasion in the mid-20th century as a quasi-communal name, as in "Geierslayer Ohligsberg.")

22. Until locks were built in the 1960s, the river was not navigable year-round. The Mosel line (*Moselstrecke*) between Koblenz and Trier was part of the "Cannons' Railway" (*Kanonenbahn*), a strategic Prussian military railway connecting Berlin with Metz, via Koblenz and Trier. The two-track line was completed in 1896, a year before the publication of Koch's book. The first railway to Trier from Saarbrücken was the Saar route in 1860; the trains stopped in Trier at a freight station on the left bank. In 1871, this route was linked to the Eifel Railway (*Eifel-Bahn*), to Cologne. The "Boozer's Line" (*Saufbähnchen*), which ran between Trier and Bullay, was built in 1903 and discontinued in 1968; the tracks ran along the river and are today a bike trail. Before 1903, the secluded station above Ürzig was the closest stop to Bernkastel for the *Moselbahn*, which included secondary lines from Wittlich to Bernkastel and from Pünderich to Traben in 1882.

ones, and the fine ones the small ones, and thus producers and merchants, who openly acknowledge the solidarity of their interests, go peacefully hand in hand.[23] On the Mosel proper—from Trier to Koblenz—there are about 80 wine merchants who operate large businesses and a somewhat larger number of merchants who deal directly with the consumers. The main wine-trading centers include the following towns: Trier, Brauneberg,[24] Mülheim, Kues, Bernkastel, Zeltingen, Traben-Trarbach,[25] Zell, Merl, Cochem-Cond, Winningen, and Koblenz. Outside the Mosel region, Cologne has a significant Mosel wine trade.

Mosel wine will continue on its path. *"Er lockelt"* is what the *Moselaner* says with witty provincialism, meaning "it entices," prompting one to take the next sip. It is, in fact, the ideal bar go-to wine. And he who knows how to look at Mosel wine's luster with a somewhat poetic glance, to him the light-green golden liquid, the fresh origin of life on the Mosel, smiles back, the fabulous romanticism of the valley shines forth, and all the blazing sunshine that enters and ripens in the grape, sparkles again in the crystal glass.

> Polish the glasses [now] 'til they shine,
> The right drop comes!
> And singing loudly
> We pull the first stopper.
> > The wine is German, the wine is good,
> > It is true Mosel vine blood.

> It is not rich and big and heavy
> Nor is it plump and opulent;
> It has the finest aroma,
> Smells like a rosebud.
> > The wine is German, the wine is good,
> > It is true Mosel vine blood.

---

23. This claim is suspiciously lacking in evidence.

24. Brauneberg, known as Dusemond before 1925, took its name from the famous hillside across the river.

25. During this time, the names were reversed: Trarbach-Traben.

So joyful as the sun shines
Down into the Mosel Valley,
And when one is about to boast,
It then does not return.
      The wine is German, the wine is good,
      It is true Mosel vine blood.

And happily under the burning sun
The wine grower plants his vines,
While cheerily the reveler's hand
Raises the Mosel glass.
      The wine is German, the wine is good,
      It is true Mosel vine blood.

So not the slightest heartbreak bothers us,
We need to keep on drinking,
Even should we out of bliss
Fall into one another's arms.
      The wine is German, the wine is good,
      It is true Mosel vine blood.[26]

26. This poem, which comprises the lyrics of a song called *Moselweinlied* (Mosel Wine Song), was written by Koch himself. It was disseminated by many other authors (von Zobeltitz, 1901; Grube, 1904; Felix Meyer, 1926; and Hotzen, 1937), without giving credit to Koch. The music was composed by Carl Wegeler, brother of Deinhard director Julius Wegeler (see note 130), and the sheet music was published at the end of the book (see facsimile), but most editions appear not to have included one.

The Winegrowing Region
of the Mosel

✦ ━━◆━━ ✦

On the sunny hillside,
>   There stand the vines so slim;
In deepest cellar vastness,
>   There lies many a cool drink.
>   Oh ray of light;
>   Oh cool wine!
Your green hills, oh river and valley,
I greet you from my heart many thousand times.
>   "Mosel Song," by Theodor Reck, 1846

T he Mosel is a true wine river from beginning to end. Grape cultivation starts close to its source in France and continues faithfully until the Mosel joins the green waves of the Rhine at Koblenz.[27]

About 9 km downriver from the small town of Pont-à-Mousson, the Mosel reaches the German border, follows it for a short stretch, and

---

27. The districts on the Mosel above Konz had almost the same area under vines as the part of the Mosel region Koch describes in this book. It is not clear what he means by "close to its source," since the nearest *vignoble de Moselle* starts about 140 km (87 miles) downstream, near the French city of Toul. The vines of the Côtes de Toul—which has more in common with winegrowing on the Meuse—lie at a distance from the Mosel. Wine from the Côtes de Toul has never been referred to as Mosel wine by the French or Germans. Downstream from Toul, the tributary Seille still has some winegrowing.

then at Novéant-sur-Moselle enters completely into German Lorraine,[28] which it leaves again between Sierck-les-Bains and Perl. Then, rushing along as a river border between Luxembourg and Germany, it rounds a curve into the Rhine Province, traversing that remarkable wine valley of which the Prussian Rhinelander is almost prouder than of his namesake Rhine.

In the French Mosel region, the production of red wine—the national drink of the French—is dominant; the German Lorraine is also known for its wine country, thanks to the cultivation of red varieties, whose best qualities, vinified to blanc de noirs, are currently much in demand as grape must for the production of sparkling wine in the large German wineries.[29] Red-wine production stops in the Lorraine commune of Thionville.[30] There, the growing of white wine takes over, which continues along the Mosel between Trier and Koblenz, and delivers racy Mosel wine, which has had an unparalleled success and is currently celebrating its triumph throughout Germany and beyond.

Already in Lorraine, a distinction is made between an upper and a lower Mosel course, and the line where the Orne River flows into the Mosel is said to be the boundary between the two.[31] But, in the Prussian Rhine Province,[32] one divides the Mosel differently. The stretch above the confluence of the Saar and Mosel rivers, near Trier, is classified as the

28. *Bezirk Lothringen*, today's French department of Moselle, belonged to the German Empire between 1871 and 1918.

29. In the 1890s, German Lorraine held about 5 percent of all the vineyards of the German Empire, although its grapes accounted for one-third of the Empire's production of sparkling wine.

30. Koch uses the German name Diedenhofen for Thionville. In his *Book of French Wines*, published in 1925, P. Morton Shand notes, "Thionville had some passable white wines. Ancy, Ars, Millery, and Jussy could be mentioned for their ordinary white wines, while Essey-la-Côte, Bayon, Liverdun, Arnaville, Pont-à-Mousson, and Pagny-sur-Moselle produced some light red wines."

31. Koch appears to be alone in making this distinction in Lorraine. His contemporary Heinrich Gerdolle, an estate owner from Metz, held the view in his 1898 article, *Der Weinbau in Lothringen*, that only the area around Sierck-les-Bains featured wines that stood apart from the rest of Lorraine, in which winegrowing was geared more toward bulk production with yields as high as 100 hl/ha versus an average yield of 35 hl/ha. Gerdolle rated as best the wines from the villages Jussy, Lessy, and Scy, all in the vicinity of Metz.

32. The Rhine Province (*Rheinprovinz*) was the westernmost province of Prussia between 1822 and 1946. Its five administrative districts (*Regierungsbezirke*) were Aachen, Düsseldorf, Cologne, Koblenz, and Trier.

Upper Mosel, followed by the Middle Mosel as far as the area of Cochem, and from there to Koblenz, the Lower Mosel.

Neither division of the course of the river corresponds to formal geographical reality, which is why both divisions reflect local tradition. Perhaps it is winegrowing that is most decisive, which is why this little book applies the generally accepted division between the Upper Mosel, Middle Mosel, and Lower Mosel in the Rhine Province.

The valley of the Middle and Lower Mosel cuts deeply into the rugged highlands of the Eifel (on the left) and the rough highlands of the Hunsrück (on the right), generally from southwest to northeast. Twisting from one side to the other, the Mosel winds through the rocky slopes.

> Why does the Mosel twist and turn so much?
> Alas, it has to reach the Rhine, the sea,
> but only wants to remain at home, to remain at home.
>
> Theobald Kerner[33]

What expatriate son or daughter of the Mosel does not get heartily homesick from these profoundly touching words! Home! Home to the fairytale land of the Mosel; below is the glittering surface of the river, up on the steep hills is the old castle, between them the fresh green color of the vines, and all outshone by the clear blue sky!

Both sides of the highlands fall steeply down to the Mosel, and where the river deviates from the generally southwest-to-northeast direction of the numerous bends, there the wall of slate along the shore insinuates itself into the path of the sunbeams, ready to unite the child of the sun, the vine, with the fertile soil. The Mosel has its meanderings predestined for winegrowing. It was recognized early on that the Mosel Valley was ideal for winegrowing. As is generally known, the Latin poet Ausonius sings in his famous idyll *Mosella* of the flourishing winegrowing on the Mosel, as he had seen with his own eyes on a trip in 370 AD.[34] It was once thought that the Roman Emperor Probus (276–282 AD) brought viticulture to the region. This view

33. Theobald Kerner (1817–1907) was a German doctor and poet who lived in Weinsberg, just east of Heilbronn.

34. Decimius Magnus Ausonius (c. 310–c. 395), whose name is preserved at Château Ausone in Saint-Émilion, was from what is modern-day Bordeaux.

was challenged when some remarkable discoveries were made in Neumagen a few years ago. Among the numerous sculptures that were excavated then and are kept today in the Trier museum,[35] some depict how the trade in wine had developed on the Mosel as early as the second half of the second century AD, which gave rise to the suspicion that winegrowing had been established there at the same time. The various fragments with depictions of ships loaded with wine casks are most interesting, and no less significant is a piece of masonry that is covered with a vine ornament.

The vines depicted on this piece of masonry display a certain similarity with the cultivation method still used today along the Mosel.[36] In the autumn of 1894, I gave a speech at the Wine Congress in Mainz on how the discoveries in Neumagen and some other evidence show that, long before the sculptures in Neumagen were made, winegrowing was brought to the Mosel not by the Romans, but by the Treveri, who already lived there. The remarkable people of this powerful tribe are often categorized as Celts, although they themselves, as Tacitus testified in his *Germania*, were keen to stress their Germanic ancestry.

How often in the late Roman Imperial era, one wonders, when a banquet in the Emperor's palace at Augusta Treverorum[37] culminated in a drinking session, might the *ministri vini die calices*[38] have filled the chalices with Mosel wine? The palace's picturesque ruins today number among Trier's top tourist attractions; and one wonders, too, whether the huge amphitheater whose remains nowadays lie on the slopes of a vineyard might even then have been nestled amid vines?

After the glory of the Roman emperors came the Migration Period, which perhaps swept away the vineyards. But winegrowing could not have been interrupted for a very long period. Already during the time of the Franks, when the tribes had settled down, winegrowing on the Mosel was protected by law under the Ripuarian Franks. According to an interesting

35. The Trier Landesmuseum, one of the most important archaeological museums in Germany, was founded in 1877. The sculpture of the Neumagen Wine Ship was discovered the next year.

36. The wooden casks depicted on these Roman fragments are also similar to those used today.

37. The City of Augustus in the land of the Treveri.

38. The Romans had a special class of servants to serve and care for wine.

book by Karl Reichelt (1886), the earliest documentation of winegrowing is from 634, when King Dagobert confirmed to Archbishop Modvald all the rights and holdings of his church, including vineyards on the Rhine, the Loire, and the Mosel.

Some villages in the administrative districts of Trier and Koblenz—also according to Reichelt—have historical evidence of winegrowing from the seventh, eighth, ninth, and tenth centuries. In the year 1000, when winegrowing was already quite extensive in Germany, the entire valley of the Middle and Lower Mosel may have been an interconnected string of vineyards. That is still the case today—the vineyards run almost uninterrupted between Trier and Koblenz.

The vineyards on either side of the Mosel are on really steep hillsides. This makes a strong impression on any person who does not come from a viticultural region and who, having imagined winegrowing—of which he knows nothing—as something that takes place on steep slopes, is always somewhat disappointed if he sees sites that are flat or on lower hills. The hillsides on the Mosel often rise so steeply that a lacework of terraces is needed to hold each hillside, so that the winegrower can plant and tend to the vine. Oh, how picturesque it is when the vines cling to each terrace along the angular cliffs, here with a small hut in the vines, there with a scene of the Stations of the Cross on the side of the road, the kind that one finds scattered in the vineyards for pilgrims.

Arduous is the work of the winegrower on steep slopes. Not only does he have to carry himself on his own legs, he must also carry everything that the vines need, no matter if the sun burns straight into his face or if the icy easterly wind from the Hunsrück whistles overhead. Were it not for the elation that it brings, the work of the winegrower would prove too much! Wine's poetry outshines the grower's labors, and that is something that he does not want to miss, whether the vintage is good or bad.

And there are so many small winegrowers whose happy, caring hands the vine requires, both in their own vineyards and those of the large estates for which they work. Nowhere else in Germany is winegrowing so much in the hands of the common man as on the Mosel, and nowhere is the parcelization of vineyards more extreme. On average, the individual landowner on the Mosel has 15 parcels. In Piesport, the average is 20, in Lieser 26, in Merl 30, and in Wolf as many as 45 parcels. A result of this parcelization is that one buys the vineyards in very small lots, in the past by square rod, and now often by square meter or by single wooden vine stake. It can happen that the individual stakes are bought in good sites for 20 or more marks, whereas in lesser sites they can be as low as 70 pfennig.

Each morgen, which is an area of 2,500 square meters, contains 2,000 to 2,500 stakes. The superior sites are less densely planted, with 2,000 stakes per morgen; the medium-quality sites a little more densely, with about 2,250 stakes; and the lower-quality sites most densely, with 2,500 stakes, and occasionally, even a little more.[39]

On the Middle and Lower Mosel—so this does not include the Upper Mosel—there are in total more than 5,650 hectares of vineyards, whose average annual yield (based on a period of many years) is between 16,000 to 17,000 *Fuder* (a *Fuder* equals 975 liters). The yield varies considerably from year to year. Some years are failures, with no more than 4 hl/ha, while a good autumn can yield 80 hl/ha.

Quantity is uncertain, as is quality, and so the success of winegrowing efforts is never really guaranteed. If the crop fails over several years, which, unfortunately, happens, the small grower will face severe hardship. In the past, when trade and transport were not so developed, the problem was even more acute than today. But even today, winegrowing is still precarious, and however high the devotion may be to the vines, equally high are the hopes for better times. Winegrowing is often not sufficient to cover basic needs. There is still one thing that cheers up the winegrower: the thought that this occupation suits the small-scale farmer better than any other agricultural activity, which enables the grower together with his family, as it were, to work for himself for a daily wage, and—what's more—in God's own fresh air, which is certainly better than earning one's bread in a musty and dusty factory. Winegrowing does not lead to enormous wealth, and the winegrower does not expect that. He, however, is and remains proud of his vines, whether or not he is blessed with a bountiful cornucopia or a disappointing harvest.

39. These figures conform to the vine density chosen by the Prussian state for its model vineyards in Ockfen, Serrig, and Avelsbach between 1897 and 1915.

Among the grape varieties planted on the Mosel, Riesling is predominant.[40] Here, in the Rhineland, Riesling, the world's finest aromatic grape, finds its greatest expression. The grape is at home on the Mosel. It needs the local soil in order to fully develop its magnificence. The slate on the hillsides, on which almost all the vines of the Middle and Lower Mosel grow, is particularly conducive to Riesling; the vines suck incalculable material from the slate, which provides for the delicious characteristics of Mosel wine. Other countries, which would like to possess such a jewel, have made many attempts to grow it, but have failed to attain the same level of quality.

The second most-planted grape variety is Elbling, also known as Elben or Kleinberger, which, in earlier times, was more widespread than even Riesling. Elbling delivers a firm, racy wine, but does not reach the heights of Riesling in terms of aroma.[41] Apart from Elbling, which grows in the chalky soil of the Upper Mosel, other varieties appear only sporadically.[42] They are fairly insignificant. Red wine is only produced in a few places.[43]

In the Mosel Valley, the poetic magic of winegrowing is combined with the captivating appeal of medieval romanticism, creating a marvelous wonderland that has no equal.[44] The ruins of the numerous castles crown

40. By this time, the best sites on slate soil had been planted to Riesling. Friedrich Wilhelm Koch (no relation to Karl Heinrich Koch) wrote that in place of Elbling most new plantings in good and even less good sites were of Riesling.

41. "On the limestone soil, mass production of wine is carried out, but this wine is—for the most part—dull, sour, and without a bouquet," wrote F.W. Koch in *Die Weine im Gebiet der Mosel und Saar* (Trier, Heinr. Stephanus, 1898).

42. The other grape varieties included Österreicher (Silvaner), Ruländer (Pinot Gris), Traminer, and Weissburgunder (Pinot Blanc).

43. Spätburgunder (Pinot Noir) was the main red variety, followed by Frühburgunder (Pinot Noir Précoce) and a little Portuguieser, according to F.W. Koch in *Weine*. A small amount of red wine was produced in Könen (Saar), Maring-Noviand, and Ürzig, as well as in Trier, Trier-Olewig, Trier-Ruwer (Ruwer-Maximin), Piesport, Lütz, and Lehmen. An auction ad from 1877 even lists a *Fuder* of red 1875 Eitelsbacher Karthäuserhofberger and a *Halbfuder* of 1875 Ockfener Herrenberger. August Trinius, in *Durch's Moseltal: Ein Wanderbuch* (Through the Mosel Valley: A Guide Book, 1897), wrote that the Mosel's red-wine production, mostly in the Lieser Valley (Maring-Noviand), was minuscule, unlike that farther north on the predominantly slate slopes of the Ahr. Spätburgunder was also produced in Assmannshausen (slate) and Ingelheim (limestone) on the Rhine, as well as in Baden.

44. The Upper Middle Rhine Valley—also part of the Rhenish Massif—with its steep slate slopes and castle ruins, has a similar appeal and is a UNESCO World Heritage Site.

the hills more picturesquely than they could do in any artist's imagination and, here and there, a part of their old luster has survived. How all the nooks and crannies of medieval culture gaze out from the small towers, bays, and cell windows glued like swallow's nests to the famous Burg Eltz, without which a true child of the Mosel cannot possibly imagine his or her homeland! Can there be any more evocative testimony to the stolid efficiency of the middle class in times gone by—for their "respectability," if I may be permitted to speak the vernacular, which always hits the nail on the head—than the massive, stout structure that is Trarbach's toll tower? And if one wants to see a genuine picture of the Mosel landscape, if one wants to understand how a village is built up on fragments of flat ground between river and hills, and how it clings to the folds of the latter, one should just take a look at a pearl of the Mosel, such as Bernkastel.

Winegrowing is more intensive on the Middle Mosel than on the Lower Mosel. On the Middle Mosel, the better sites are adjacent to one another, but on the Lower Mosel they are more isolated. The border between the Middle and Lower Mosel is not exactly defined. Some locate the border at Traben-Trarbach, where the administrative district of Trier borders the administrative district of Koblenz. Others consider the border to be farther downriver in the area of Alf, while others still see Cochem as the border. Between Trier and Cochem, the frequent twists and turns of the Mosel are blessings for winegrowing. Below Cochem, the Mosel takes a straighter course down to Koblenz. Therefore, I think that those who assume the border is at Cochem are right.

The wines of the Upper Mosel are not generally regarded as *true* Mosel wines; they form their own type.[45] The following chapter provides some details about the wine villages of the Middle Mosel—which includes the lower part of the Saar—and the Lower Mosel.

45. The area was also called the *Muschelkalkgebiet* (shell-bearing limestone region) or *Kalkweingebiet* (limestone wine region), with Germany on the right bank (until Oberbillig) and Luxembourg on the left, and had scarcely any Riesling, with the notable exception of Wormeldange. According to F.W. Koch, the chalky soils of the Upper Mosel were best known for bulk wine, reaching 80 hl/ha in some vintages. Like the wines of Alsace, the wines of Luxembourg started to regain quality only after the First World War. Improvement on the German bank is more recent.

The Wine Villages of the Mosel

✦———✦———✦

I hear a vintner singing,
The forest creek roars, the castles come closer,
Along the river dances,
From village to village my small boat.
  Drink and sing!
The cup fizzes from Mosel wine,
And where its tone sounds,
There my anchor is dropped.

Gustav Pfarrius, "Moselwein," 1860

Although, as has been said, there is only one true Mosel wine, it can be helpful to divide the lengthy area of production into different sections in order to provide a better overview. The geographical distinction in the Rhine Province between the Middle and Lower Mosel is also used with respect to viticulture. Both in terms of quantity and quality of the wines, the Middle Mosel takes precedence over the Lower Mosel. As things stand now, one can easily have a clear enough picture of the production area of the Lower Mosel,[46] but that is not the case for the Middle Mosel, which one better divides into different winegrowing areas. Since the Saar region belongs to the Middle Mosel, we will first

---

46. For more on the different subregions of the Mosel, see Lars Carlberg's essay.

deal with the Saar, and then continue with the valley of the Middle Mosel, divided at Piesport, into two sections. This gives us the following outline: 1. The Saar Region; 2. The Mosel from the Mouth of the Saar to Piesport; 3. The Mosel from Piesport to Cochem; 4. The Mosel from Cochem to Koblenz.

The Saar Region

At Konz, the Saar empties into the Mosel. The principal area of production for Saar wine is the Saar River's right bank (where the vineyards of Konz are singularly regarded as belonging to the Mosel). If a line is drawn from Saarburg to Trier, then the triangle whose points are Saarburg, Konz, and Trier represents roughly that blessed little fleck of earth on which the very famous Saar wines ripen. Winegrowing is more limited beyond the Saarburg–Konz line and onto the Saar's left bank.[47] The area is small and the winegrowing villages are few, but they have certainly learned how to make a name for themselves.

In total, these Saar vineyards add up to about 490 ha, which, on average, give a yearly production of 1,500 *Fuder*.[48] The production on the Saar contributes only one-tenth of the total production of the Middle and Lower Mosel, but its qualitative significance becomes immediately clear when one considers its success at the great Trier wine auctions. For instance, a total of 1,567½ *Fuder* were auctioned from the 1893 vintage. Of these, 646½ were Saar wines, which brought in an average of 3,547 marks, while the remaining 921 *Fuder* brought in an average of 2,946 marks.

Saar wines are generally credited with displaying the most noble of Riesling bouquets, even more than do those of the Mosel Valley. They are also leaner, more ethereal, and indeed even lighter in color, but otherwise generally of genuine Mosel character.

While the whole Saar Valley displays a certain similarity to that of the Mosel in its undulations, winegrowing on the Saar takes place on

47. The main left-bank vineyards, from south to north, are in Saarburg, Ayl, and Wawern.

48. The vineyard area today is about 790 ha.

less steep sites.[49] The vine flourishes in slate soils on gentle slopes, which are, for the most part, not situated immediately adjacent to the Saar, but, rather, in side valleys. Another difference in winegrowing on the Saar is that the vineyard holdings are not as fragmented as on the Mosel. The vineyards of the Saar are to a greater extent in the hands of large producers.

Along the Saar Valley, the wine villages are arrayed as follows, from the upper to the lower river: Staadt,[50] near Saarburg, on the left bank; the good site of Saarstein, in the district of Serrig, on the right bank;[51] Saarburg on the left;[52] Beurig and Irsch on the right; Niederleuken left;[53] Ockfen, where the State has now planted vines,[54] right, nearby, the splendid sites of Bockstein[55]

49. There are several notable exceptions, such as Saarburger Kupp and Fuchs, as well as Wiltinger Gottesfuss and Kanzemer Altenberg (then known as "Canzemerberg").

50. Staadt—today called Kastel-Staadt—is located across from Serrig on the left bank of the Saar. In the 1890s, M.J. Keller auctioned his Staadter or Maximin-Staadter wines by the *Fuder*; today, the site is called Maximiner Prälat. His 1893s were described as "full-bodied wines with a pronounced lively Saar bouquet, crystal clear, and completely dry, which was not always the case with other '93 wines."

51. The other steep-slope vineyards in Serrig, such as Würtzberg, purchased by Frau Wwe. E. Puricelli in 1897, and those of the Royal Prussian State Domain (now owned by Markus Molitor), were cleared of woods and planted to vines starting around 1900. (Serriger Herrenberg, adjacent to Würtzberg, was planted a couple years later.) But a small vineyard on the south-facing slope at Saarstein was already in cultivation in 1828. M.F. Hansen produced 14 *Fuder* of "Saarsteiner" in 1893.

52. By 1890, the main vineyard areas of Saarburg comprised Schlossberg, an east-to-southeast-facing slope adjacent to the castle ruin, and today's Saarburger Rausch, which, since 2011, encompasses the former *Einzellagen* Saarburger Antoniusbrunnen and Bergschlösschen, once called Mühlberg. See page 72.

53. Niederleuken, misspelled "Niederlenken" on Clotten's 1890 map, refers to the post-1971 *Einzellagen* Saarburger Kupp, Stirn, and Fuchs. The pre-1971 sites were named Niederleukener Kupp, Stirn (*Gewann* In der Stirn), and Fuchs. (Formerly, the old site names included Lay, Jungenwald, Seifen, Kreuzberg, and Altenberg.) On the first and last editions of Clotten's tax map, Stirn, which means "brow," was rated the best site and marked in light red, the rest of the vineyards in beige. Immediately downstream on the narrow end of the same steep slope and perched on a cliff, with an east-to-southeast exposition, are the cadastral place names Auf Schonfels (a part of Fuchs), Schonfels, and Lambertskirch. (The latter two are in the commune of Ayl, and Schonfels can technically be labeled as "Ayler Kupp.")

54. In 1896, the Prussian government established the Royal State Domains as model wineries to school winegrowers in better methods. Vines were planted first in Ockfen (Heppenstein and Bockstein) and later in Avelsbach (Hammerstein and Rotlei), nearby Trier, and Serrig (Vogelsang and Schiessberg). Another Prussian state-owned model winery established around 1900 was on the Nahe in Niederhausen-Schlossböckelheim, now privatized and renamed Gut Hermannsberg.

55. Since 1983, Ockfener Bockstein refers to the entire hillside. Before then, the sites and later

and Geisberg;[56] Ayl left, a bit off the river, with the good site of Neuberg;[57] Biebelhausen left; Schoden right; Wiltingen right, with the nearby famous sites of Scharzhofberg and Scharzberg.[58] Kanzem left,[59] with the vineyards on the right side, among them the good site of Kelterberg;[60] Wawern left, a bit off the river, with the excellent site of Herrenberg; Hamm right; Filzen right. The last of these villages is Könen, on the left, where a popular red wine is made.[61]

The valley that stretches east from Wiltingen, the so-called Oberemmel Valley,[62] is also very important. The valley cuts a wide swath through this

Einzellagen included Ockfener Kupp, Herrenberg, Heppenstein, Bockstein, Zickelgarten, and Neuwies. See page 68.

56. Along with having replanted large parts of the south-facing slopes in Wawern (Goldberg), Oberemmel (the former Junkerberg), and other villages of the Saar, Van Volxem is now recultivating ca. 14 ha in the once famous Geisberg, a steep slope to the east of Bockstein—where Van Volxem has also taken over many vineyards in recent years—and rich in quartzite-laden sandstone. See page 70.

57. Neuberg is a site within Ayler Kupp and was at one time a new part of the hill planted to vines, hence the name "new hill." See page 67.

58. The "new" Scharzberg vineyard—primarily situated on the slope to the east of Scharzhof in the direction of Oberemmel—is now part of the enlarged 28.1-ha Scharzhofberg (which, technically, is *einzellagenfrei*, or not designated as an *Einzellage*). See page 73.

59. Frau Wwe. Jul. Weissbach, who inherited the wine estate now known as von Othegraven, located in Kanzem, offered yearly at auction her wines from two large parcels in the 18.7-ha *Einzellage* Kanzemer Altenberg (Canzemerberg) as either "Canzemer" or "Canzemer-Herrenberger." Bischöfliches Priesterseminar and Vereinigte Hospitien also auctioned wines from this imposing steep slope, which has a ferruginous slate soil and includes the 0.4-ha site "Härker," or Hörecker (*Gewann* Im Hohrecker).

60. Koch is referring to the site of Kelterberg (*Gewann* Im Kelterberg) depicted in dark red on Clotten's map. It is located in a section of today's *Einzellage* Wiltinger Klosterberg next to Wiltinger Gottefuss. Just downstream from Kelterberg is Wiltinger Kupp (*Gewann* In der Kupp), colored light red. Norbert le Gallais in Dommeldingen owned 2 ha on the dome-shaped, south-facing slope, now known as Wiltinger braune Kupp. His wines were cellared in Kanzem and sold at auction in Trier. Le Gallais is now part of the 16 ha of vineyards farmed by Egon Müller. Bischöfliches Priesterseminar and von Othegraven also have vineyards in the famous Wiltinger Kupp. Two other dark-red flecks on Clotten's map identify Fasel and Volz (also spelled "Vols"), enclaves of today's Wiltinger Klosterberg and Braunfels, respectively.

61. The red vines were grubbed up in 1920. Frau Wwe. Jul. Gensterblum offered her bottle-aged Pinot Noirs from Schabberg and Nonnenberg in 100-bottle packs at the Trier auctions, including one *Fuder* of 1892 Schabberger Auslese. These "Cönener" red wines were described in an article on the 1898 Wine Congress as being similar to those of the Burgundy's Côte d'Or.

62. The Oberemmel Valley, which extends from Oberemmel to Wiltingen, is half of a wide U-shaped side valley that, as Koch points out, geologists widely theorize represents a former

landscape, which the geologist Heinrich Grebe presumed to constitute the former riverbed of an arm of the Mosel that flowed through here in prehistoric times. Along this stretch, one will find the villages of Oberemmel, with the renowned sites of Rosenberg,[63] Agritiusberg (at the church), Raul, Lautersberg, and Junkerberg;[64] Krettnach;[65] as well as Ober- and Niedermennig with the excellent sites of Euchariusberg[66] and Zuckerberg,[67] respectively.

Wiltingen, with about 100 ha, is the largest winegrowing commune; then follows Oberemmel with about 70 ha; Ockfen with 40 ha; Kanzem with about 37.5 ha; Ayl and Wawern with about 30 ha each; and other villages with a winegrowing area of less than 30 ha.

riverbed of the Mosel. The other half of the valley is the Konzer Tälchen ("the little valley of Konz"), which includes Konz, Niedermennig, Obermennig, and Krettnach. (In the 1890s, and even today, it was also thought by some to be a former bed of the Saar, like other looping side valleys in Ayl–Wawern and Irsch–Ockfen.)

63. In the 1890s, Oberemmeler Rosenberg referred exclusively to a well-known south-facing hillside just west of the village and listed as "Rosenkamm" on Clotten's map. Both von Hövel and von Kesselstatt have holdings in this site.

64. Like Agritiusberg and Rosenberg, Raul is a largely forgotten but once highly rated site in Oberemmel. Adjacent to Raul, on the same slope, are the old sites (from west to east): Lautersberg, Hütte, Elzerberg, and Junkerberg (a part of today's *Einzellage* Oberemmeler Altenberg). On Clotten's 1890 map, the area between Raul and Elzerberg is shown in dark red without gaps. The site name "Hütte" is first listed on the 1906 edition. The post-1971 5.8-ha *Einzellage* Oberemmeler Hütte, solely owned by von Hövel, includes both Lautersberg and Elzerberg. In 1898, Frau Wwe. Jos. Grach owned 11.25 ha in Oberemmel (Hütte, Lautersberg, Elzerberg, Agritiusberg, Rosenberg, and Junkerberg) and Wiltingen (Scharzberg); von Hövel now has 21.5 ha of vineyards. See page 72.

65. "Krettnach" refers to the original south-facing slope of the *Einzellage* Krettnacher Altenberg, which is listed as "Crettnacherberg" on the 1906 edition of Clotten's map, a part of which is marked dark red. The wines were auctioned as "Crettnacher." Diabase veins run through this slate slope, particularly noticeable on the prime western flank (called Silberberg in the mid-20th century) in the place names Auf dem Hölzchen and Ober Schäfershaus.

66. The historic Euchariusberg hillside, marked dark red on Clotten's map, is also known as Großschock (or Gross Schock). See page 69.

67. Zuckerberg was an old designation for the main hill, above Niedermennig, in today's *Einzellage* Niedermenniger Herrenberg. In a narrower sense, Herrenberg refers to the western half and Zuckerberg to the eastern half of this south-facing slope that constitutes the core Herrenberg. The adjoining *Gewanne* Im Herrenberg, Im Zuckerberg, and Im Langenberg, all three owned by von Kesselstatt and once leased to Markus Molitor, are located in the heart of this hillside, with its iron-rich gray-clayey slate soil. In 1881, F. Simon of Roscheiderhof began to plant vines in the bordering Niedermenniger Sonnenberg, which has a similar soil. He was a son of the owner of Simonbräu (today known as Bitburger); a former press house, Simonshof, built in 1897, sits atop the hill. Before 1881, the only area planted to vines in what is now the *Einzellage* Niedermenniger Sonnenberg stretched from Im Kleinschock (named "Schock" on Clotten's 1868 map), just north of Euchariusberg, to the forested hilltop Unter den Röderchen.

The best vineyards among those mentioned above have made such a name for themselves that even without the benefit of village attribution[68] their wines have managed to make their way throughout the world.

The Mosel from the Mouth of the Saar to Piesport

About halfway between the mouth of the Saar and Piesport, hidden behind an immense apple orchard, lies the large, prosperous wine town of Schweich, as a gatekeeper to the narrow Mosel Valley, which, from here on cuts deeply into the Rhenish Massif, making its way to the Rhine in countless characteristic twists and turns. But upstream from Schweich, the valley stretches out to 3 km wide for 20 km until it reaches the Saar. And almost in the middle of the lush landscape of this river plain, the towers of Trier rise to greet us. This part of the Mosel is called the Trier Valley, whose entire length, all the way to Schweich, one can take in at a single glance from the church tower of Konz. But all the splendors upstream and downstream are much lovelier if one gazes out from the rocky cliff's edge at Pallien, immediately opposite Trier.[69]

If the Trier Valley and the Mosel Valley below Schweich offer different scenery, so, too, is each sector's viticultural character different. In the Mosel Valley, downriver from Schweich, the vineyards extend right down to the edge of the water, whereas in the Trier Valley they tend more often to recede from the shoreline.

Upriver from Schweich, winegrowing on the left bank is insignificant. At Trier, only the two sites of Irminen and Augenschein[70] are worth

68. In Koch's time, some of the most prominent Saar vineyards marketed without village attribution were Scharzhofberg, Scharzberg, Bockstein, Geisberg, and Euchariusberg. Scharzhof is a part of the commune of Wiltingen, but Wiltingen is omitted on the labels to this day, as Scharzhofberg is not recognized as an *Einzellage*. So instead of labeling the wine as "Wiltinger Scharzhofberg," producers are permitted to label it as either "Scharzhofberg" or "Scharzhofberger."

69. Koch is referring to the red sandstone cliff below Villa Weisshaus and opposite the fishing quarter of Zurlauben, both of which are designated on Clotten's map.

70. Irminen, in Trier-West, is no longer planted to vines. Farther downstream, Augenschein, now officially named Trierer Augenscheiner, features red sandstone and is a *monopole* site of Vereinigte Hospitien, which, in Koch's day, also had a vineyard in Irminen.

mentioning, the latter of which extends exceptionally close to the Mosel. The name Augenschein is said to have come about because it caught the eye of monks across the river in St. Mary's Abbey.[71] Konz, situated on the right bank, has rather significant vineyards, and immediately afterwards comes the city of Trier, with almost 125 ha of vineyards. Here the famous Thiergärtner[72] and Avelsbacher[73] are situated at Olewig and Kürenz, respectively. Pichter[74] and Neuberg[75] are also among the better sites.

Not far from Trier, at the village of Ruwer, the eponymous tributary flows into the Mosel from the right. Fine examples of viticulture commence high upstream in Waldrach[76] and continue downstream past Kasel and Mertesdorf to Eitelsbach, where the Karthäuserhof is on the right and Grünhaus on the left. Kaseler,[77] Karthäuserhofberger,[78] and Grünhäuser

71. St. Marien, one of Trier's four Benedictine monasteries, also owned Scharzhof and planted vines there in 1767. The French confiscated St. Marien in 1794, initially utilizing it as a military hospital and later as barracks. After the Congress of Vienna, it was the quarters of the highest-ranking officer of the Prussian garrison, which is why it was called Exzellenzhaus (now better known as Exhaus) in common parlance.

72. In recent times, much of Thiergarten's steep slope has been unused, whereas the valley floor has been planted with vines. Terraces now traverse the hillside, and von Nell has replanted it.

73. "Avelsbacher" refers to the *Einzellagen* Avelsbacher Altenberg (slate and diabase) and Herrenberg. A little farther up the valley on an adjacent slope, the Royal Prussian State Domain began to clear oak coppices and plant Riesling vines in the expansive "Neuavelsberg," in what is today Avelsbacher Hammerstein, using prison labor in 1900. Domäne Avelerberg was 30 ha.

74. Pichter is a hillside vineyard located directly behind the main train station in Trier-Kürenz and is now part of St. Maximiner Kreuzberg. Vereinigte Hospitien auctioned the wines as "Tonnenpichter."

75. Neuberg, marked dark red, is a prime vineyard area on a south-facing slope in Trier-Olewig. Vereinigte Hospitien auctioned the wines as "Olewig-Neuberger." A neighboring top site is Vollmühl, and to the east is Retzgrub.

76. Sommerau and Morscheid, the first wine villages on the Ruwer, were yet to be listed on the 1890 edition of Clotten's map. At the time, Waldrach was then the uppermost village with vines.

77. The significant vineyard areas on the Ruwer are the hillsides, facing south, in Kasel, at Karthäuserhof, and at Grünhaus. "Caseler" wines often issued from Herrenberg and adjacent Kehrnagel, which was the south-facing slope upstream from Kasel and marked dark red on Clotten's map. Most of the better-known Kasel sites were in what is today the *Einzellage* Kaseler Nies'chen: Hitzlay, Taubenberg, and Pichter. Hitzlay now designates an *Einzellage* that lies above and to the east of Nies'chen, including the old sites Höchst and Coles. The 1906 edition of Clotten's map also includes Steininger, which, along with Pichter and Taubenberg, compose the area colored dark red on the hillside rising behind "Casel." Top producers included von Kesselstatt and von Beulwitz.

78. In Eitelsbach, the dark-red sector of the esteemed Karthäuserhofberg, with its iron-

are stars in a long line of famous Mosel wine names. At the Trier spring auction in 1896, two *Fuder* of the 1893 Maximiner Grünhäuser Herrenberger were sold at 11,010 and 12,750 marks, respectively, which are the highest prices ever paid for any Mosel wine. Frankish King Dagobert I (died 639) gave Grünhaus,[79] earlier called *ad valles*, to the Trier monastery of St. Maximin,[80] and this was affirmed by the Holy Roman Emperor Otto I (912–973) on January 7, 966. It was thereby established that a prayer should be offered for the king on the first day of each month, and that the monks should then take a healthy draught of Grünhäuser. Curiously, wines of the Ruwer Valley are referred to as *"Heckenweine."*[81] The valley is easily accessible from the rail line to Hermeskeil.[82]

Between the Ruwer and Mosel, downstream from Schweich, the following villages still support winegrowing: Kenn, Fastrau, Niederfell, and Oberfell.

rich gray-clayey slate soil, is identified as Kronenberg, considered the best subsite of the slope. The hill is called Karthäuserberg, as on Clotten's map. In 1897, Frau Wwe. Rautenstrauch ran the 15-ha Karthäuserhof, which was founded by the Carthusian order of St. Alban in Trier in 1335. (In 1674, during the Franco-Dutch War, St. Alban and other convents outside the city walls were razed by French troops. A new Carthusian monastery, St. Bruno, was built in Merzlich, today's Konz-Karthaus.)

79. In 1882, Carl Ferdinand Stumm, a Prussian coal and steel industrialist from the Saarland, purchased Maximin Grünhaus for the price of 600,000 marks. After Stumm was ennobled in 1888, the estate became known as Freiherrlich von Stumm-Halberg'sche Rittergutsverwaltung Grünhaus. See page 71.

80. Founded in the 4th century, at the time of its dissolution and the confiscation of its property by a French consular decree in 1802, the Benedictine St. Maximin's Abbey in Trier was the largest landowner in the greater Mosel region. Subsequently its buildings were employed for various purposes, and most were knocked down around 1900. Only the archway and the church remain, now used as a school gym and concert hall.

81. Literally, "hedge wines." In the 19th century, "hedge wines" described wines from vineyards in side valleys in and around Trier—in particular, Ruwer wines (Grünhäuser, Eitelsbacher, Kaseler) but also Saar wines (Scharzhofberger, Oberemmeler, Krettnacher). The hedges were made of *Lohhecke*, coppiced oak, which grows in much of the region, along with other areas of the Rhenish Slate Mountains. The bark had been used by the thriving local leather-tanning industry, but during the height of Mosel wine, as the price of oak bark fell and the price of vineyard land dramatically rose, the trees were cut down for vineyards, especially on privileged south-facing slate slopes in side valleys, such as at Geisberg in Ockfen and at Kohlberg (or Kohlenberg, later named Dominikanerberg) in Kasel. Villa Keller, in Saarburg, once belonged to Max Keller, whose family had built a tannery next to the villa and owned woods and vineyards in Ockfen, including Bockstein and Geisberg. In Trier, the traditional tannery Joh. Rendenbach jr. announced in October 2021 that it would close its doors in 2022 after having stayed true to time-honored methods since 1871. It supplied natural high-quality oak-tanned leather soles for many of the world's best shoemakers.

82. The first section of the Hochwaldbahn or Ruwertalbahn railway line between Trier and Hermeskeil opened in 1889. The line was terminated in 1998 and is today a bicycle path.

At Schweich, the scenery suddenly changes. The valley closes tightly, the vineyards on the left bank are situated closer to the Mosel, accompanying it past Longuich—which, however, lies on the right bank—and then further, past Longen, Lörsch, and Mehring to Pölich. At Longuich, the vines cover the slope of the high Schückberg,[83] whose summit was infamous as a witches' dance floor, but is nowadays famed as an observation point. On the right lies Riol. Directly opposite Mehring—rebuilt after the conflagration of June 8, 1840—the ancient wine road to Birkenfeld climbs up the hill at "Cowstantinopel," as local wit has dubbed those buildings associated with the adjacent pastures.

Between Pölich and Schleich, the vineyards jump over to the right bank and stay on that side as far as Detzem, then come back to the left bank at Ensch, and from there, via Thörnich (which is on the other side),[84] reach Klüsserath, which produces a lot of wine, and whose name (owing to the extent of this village's riverfront) has become a byword for sheer length;[85] it produces a lot of wine. Then follows Köwerich on the right, but with vineyards on the left, and Leiwen to the right with viticulture on both sides, the best sites to the left. Opposite lies the Laurentiusberg,[86] whose vines belong mainly to producers in Trittenheim, situated where the Mosel takes a sharp bend; it has both left and right the most substantial vineyards in this part of the Mosel with almost 100 ha, among them many excellent sites. Trittenheim is known not only for its winegrowing but also for being the birthplace of Johannes Tritheim, or Trithemius (1462–1515), abbot of

---

83. Schückberg presumably refers to the large hillside of today's *Einzellagen* Longuicher Herrenberg and Maximiner Herrenberg, which is marked dark red on Clotten's map.

84. The best site in Thörnich and one of the most underrated sites in the Mosel Valley is the majestic, craggy, steep south-facing Ritsch, which includes the core *Gewann* In der Ritsch. In a narrow side valley, Schneidersberg (*Gewann* Im Schneidersberg), where the slope faces more to the west, was designated as a new planting on Clotten's 1906 map and is a part of the expanded *Einzellage* Thörnicher Ritsch.

85. *"So lang wie Klüsserath"*—"as long as Klüsserath"—is still a Mosel expression.

86. Laurentiusberg refers to the hillside on the left bank of the Mosel opposite Leiwen. The slope's tail end includes the place names Im Laurentiusberg and Im Lorenziusberg, both of which are in the commune of Trittenheim and part of the post-1971 *Einzellage* Trittenheimer Apotheke. (The original Apotheke is on the steep right-bank slope opposite Trittenheim.) Other sites located on the hillside known as Laurentiusberg include Trittenheimer Felsenkopf (solely owned by Josef Milz) and a small part of today's *Einzellage* Leiwener Laurentiuslay.

the Benedictine Abbey of Sponheim and a renowned medieval historian. Mosel author Karl Hessel has said of Tritheim: "Despite their fables and unreliability, his annals have bequeathed us especially many anecdotes from earlier centuries, anecdotes that spiced up the history lessons of our fond youth, such as the legend of the loyal women of Weinsberg."[87]

The imposing village of Neumagen—Noviomagus under the Romans—with houses genially peeking out from amid luxuriant gardens, is also situated in the middle of vineyards, a number of which are excellent. This is where the Roman road from Bingen over the Hunsrück reached the Mosel and here the aforementioned poet Ausonius, after a trek through the wilds of the Soonwald, caught his first glimpse of that wine valley to which he erected an abiding monument with his lovely idyll *Mosella*. Here stood the fortifications of Emperor Constantine, and it was here those ancient sculptures were unearthed that silently yet eloquently tell us about Mosel wine of almost 2,000 years ago.

The conclusion of this stretch of the Mosel—a splendid one—is the set of vineyards in the side valley of the Dhron, which, after receiving the waters of the Little Dhron (known also as the Dhrönchen), clamorously rushes from the hills with as much vigor as any high-forest stream and flows into the Mosel at Neumagen. In its upper course, the Little Dhron flows by the Dhronecken Castle, the alleged ancestral seat of the two *Tronegaere* (the Dhroneckers), grim Hagen and his impetuous brother Danckwart, of whom the "Nibelungenlied" sings. Dhroner Hofberg is a renowned name on Mosel labels,[88] and viticulture in the village of Dhron, at more than 75 ha, is not insignificant. Dhron once belonged to the Principality of Wagram. Established by Napoleon's grace expressly for his Marshal Berthier,[89] this dominion managed only a fleeting existence. When the

87. After the town's fortifications fell to a siege in the 12th century, the women of Weinsberg—promised safe passage along with whatever they could carry on their backs—were said to have shouldered their menfolk and spirited them to safety down steep slopes that are coincidentally considered today to be among Württemberg's better vineyard sites (and are among its most dramatic).

88. Dhroner Hofberg (sometimes also spelled Throner Hofberg) is on the right bank of the Mosel in a side valley. On Clotten's 1890 map, the prime dark-red section, just below the place name In der Sengerei, is the *Gewann* Im Hofberg, which once belonged to the Tholey Abbey in Saarland. Im Hofberg is owned by Bischöfliches Priesterseminar, which annually auctioned its *Fuder* of "Dhronhofberger" in Trier during Koch's time.

89. Louis-Alexandre Berthier (1753–1815) was the Prince of Wagram (from 1809), Sovereign

French withdrew *en masse*, Berthier sold the estates in Dhron that Napoleon had given him and transferred the proceeds to the State Treasury. *Chapeau!* The winegrowing sector from the mouth of the Saar to Piesport (but not including the vineyards of that village itself, which commences the next stretch we will consider) comprises approximately 1,050 ha of vines, from which about 3,000 *Fuder* of wine are harvested annually—i.e., almost a fifth of the total production of the Middle and Lower Mosel.

This sector gravitates toward Trier, whose renown as a wine city nearly outshines its ancient fame as an imperial city of the Roman Empire. Mighty ruins bear witness to this past imperial glory. But when one strolls through the remarkable and well-preserved Porta Nigra, one is captivated not just by recollections of Roman antiquity, but also by the thought that the northern route out of the city and into the blessed Mosel wine valley passed through this gate. Trier has a good viticultural school and a substantial wine trade. Its reputation as a wine city is owed, however, to the great wine auctions at which—to the extent not sold privately—the finest production of the Middle Mosel and the lower part of the Saar is traded. The completely free competition among experts to acquire the top growths represents an instance of highly credible price benchmarking, and chance plays no role, when the value of wines is established at these auctions. The quantity that goes under the hammer is not what is most important. As noted in the previous chapter, from the 1893 vintage only 1,567½ *Fuder* were auctioned—and spread over two occasions at that: in the spring of 1895 and in the spring of 1896. Then again, more than 5 million marks were paid for them. According to the table published by the bookseller Friedrich Lintz in Trier,[90] the results from the

---

Prince of Neuchâtel, as well as French Marshal and Vice-Constable of the Empire and Chief of Staff under Napoleon I.

90. Fr. Lintz'schen Buchhandlung was a book publisher and bookseller in Trier owned by the Lintz family, who also possessed vineyards in Wawern on the Saar, particularly in Wawerner Herrenberg (*Gewann* Großer Herrenberg), colored light red on Clotten's 1868 map. Today, von Othegraven is the sole owner and producer of Wawerner Herrenberger. Apart from the auction outcomes, the Lintzes released other wine publications—notably, F.W. Koch's *Weine* and the second edition (1890) of Clotten's *Weinbau-Karte*. The firm was split among three brothers in 1898. The eldest brother, Jakob Lintz (1845–1918), remained active in both winegrowing and publishing and continued to publish the auction results. He also published Eduard Markworth's map of the Lower Mosel in 1897, the fourth edition of Clotten's map of the Saar and Mosel in 1906, and Henri Schliep's *Mosel & Sauer* map of Luxembourg and the Upper Mosel in 1910.

1893 vintage[91] were as follows:

Fuder of 975 liters	Growth	Average price per Fuder in marks	Fuder of 975 liters	Growth	Average price per Fuder in marks
	a) Mosel			b) Saar	
17	Augenscheiner	1,753	30	Ayler	2,942
39½	Avelsbacher	3,095	64½	Bocksteiner	4,020
41	Bernkasteler	3,291	49	Kanzemer	2,780
15	Brauneberger	4,483	13½	Feilser	3,107
9	Dhroner Hofberger	2,833	22	Geisberger	4,393
29	Erdener	3,138	141½	Oberemmelerthaler (Agritiusberger, Rauler, Rosenberger, Euchariusberger, etc.)	3,087
39½	Geierslayer	2,497			
69	Graacher	2,624			
33½	Josephshöfer	4,443			
16	Irminer	846	52	Ockfener	3,652
35	Lieserer Niederberger	3,045	25	Saarburger	1,236
34	Mattheiser	1,637	46½	Scharzberger	4,047
15	Mehringer	1,439	70½	Scharzhofberger	5,504
11	Olewiger	1,665	18½	Staadter	2,466
22	Ohligsberger	3,121	31	Wawerner	4,215
25½	Pichter	1,455	82½	Wiltinger	3,145
74	Piesporter	3,493	646½	Fuder avg.	3,547
12	Thiergärtner	4,416			
21	Trarbacher	1,253		c) Ruwer	
26	Trittenheimer	2,211	83	Eitelsbacher-Karthäuserhofberger	3,391
21½	Ürziger	2,132	80	Grünhäuser	4,041
52	Zeltinger	3,682	100½	Kaseler	2,536
657½	Fuder avg.	2,818	263½	Fuder avg.	3,263

91. The 1893 vintage was considered great but had early botrytis (and more Auslese wines), whereas 1892 was more classic. As a point of reference, a 612-liter *Halbstück* of 1893 Marco-brunner auctioned for an incredible 16,500 marks in Kloster Eberbach on May 29, 1895, much more than any Mosel wine.

The wines of the 1895 vintage sold at the 1897 spring auctions achieved per *Fuder*:

	Fuder	Average price in marks
Mosel	611	2,465
Saar	270	3,510
Ruwer	122	2,942

The enthusiastic potential buyers, pressed tightly inside the auction hall,[92] follow the bidding with mounting suspense. And when the best wines reach all-time high prices, a storm of applause breaks out that sets the walls rumbling. The producer thought not of vile Mammon when he rendered a noble essence of this sort captured through laborious selection. Rather, he thought only of the glory. Pride at his having succeeded in weaving a new, fresh sprig into the Mosel's wreath of glory causes the excitement of those assembled to seek release in tumultuous applause.

The Mosel from Piesport to Cochem

We have now arrived at the midpoint of the Mosel's production area. The oft-observed phenomenon that the midsection of a winegrowing region is distinguished not just by its volume but also for its quality makes itself especially apparent on the Mosel. A lot of wine is grown between Piesport and Cochem, and good and preeminent vineyard sites are so numerous that they literally press against one another.

The Bernkastel area represents the heart of the Middle Mosel. Gazing across the Mosel landscape from the bridge at Bernkastel, the eye comes to rest on numerous famous vineyard sites, though the twisting Mosel Valley tightly reins in visibility. At such times, one wishes one could rise into the air, so as to gaze across all the vines that range ever more densely from the heights down to the edge of the river, whose silver ribbon appends one loop to the next. It is as if one vineyard would like to push the other ones

92. The grand hall of the Katholischer Bürgerverein (Catholic Civic Society) was part of a large complex of buildings on the site of today's Europahalle and what is now a Best Western hotel, between the Viehmarkt and Kaiserstraße. It was destroyed in December 1944 by Royal Air Force bombing; only the foundation and cellar remained.

aside: "Give way! I do things better here than you do!" Everywhere the liveliest competition, but the whole life of the valley revolves around wine.

This stretch of the river begins with the vineyards of Piesport. Almost in a semicircle, open to the south so that the sun can burn into steep, rocky sites, the roughly 125 ha of vineyards at Piesport and Niederemmel (also called Emmel)—which, together with Müstert and Reinsport, constitute a single parish—drape themselves over the left bank of a bow in the Mosel. What more can be said to the glory of Piesport wines,[93] since they themselves know how to speak so sonorously and distinctly! Things in Piesport were not always as they are now. In the 18th century, it was believed one would do well to replace the noble Riesling grape with some other variety. But adversity is the school of wisdom! Riesling has recaptured this terroir tailor-made for it, and now nobody imagines that another variety could do better.

Between Minheim, on the left (with its Rosenberg vineyard), and Wintrich, on the right, the vineyards jump over to the right bank, where we find the excellent Ohligsberg site—named for a chapel "on the 'Mount of Olives,'"—and the Neuberg site, in a small side valley, which both produce outstanding wines. Also worth mentioning for its good wines is Hof Geierslay.[94] Via Kesten, with the Paulinsberg on the left, we move on to Monzel. The Brauneberg hill rises up from here, its slopes completely covered with vines, which in a good year yield about 800 *Fuder*

93. The best sites in Piesport included, among others, Falkenberg, Weer (also spelled Wehr), and Pichter, the only three listed on Clotten's 1868 and 1890 maps. Pichter is located just above the village. Falkenberg and Weer are closer to the hamlet of Ferres. Weer (*Gewann* Im Weer) is incorporated in today's *Einzellage* Piesporter Domherr; right above is Falkenberg (*Gewann* Im Falkenberg)—which borders the 0.8-ha *Einzellage* Piesporter Schubertslay (*Gewann* In der Rötsch) to the east—and is now a part of the much expanded post-1971 *Einzellage* Piesporter Goldtröpfchen (64.5 ha), whereas the *Einzellage* Piesporter Falkenberg is more or less the upper half of the grand Piesport slope (see glossary).

94. Hof Geierslay, which today houses Weingut Geierslay, is a cluster of buildings located at the site of an ancient boat landing and was then one of two bases of operation for Adolf Böcking (the other being in Trarbach). Böcking and his in-law successors, the Huesgen family, were both based in Traben-Trarbach and farmed prime portions of Wintrich's Ohligsberg (i.e., the south slope of "Oligsberg") and Neuberg, whose names regularly appear on auction lists of this period. (Eduard Puricelli and his successor von Schorlemer were the other prominent, wealthy landholders farming Wintrich's top sites.) On "Geierslay" as a site name, see note 21. Confusingly, the quartz-rich slate soil of Neuberg corresponds roughly with the post-1971 *Einzellage* that was given the name Wintricher Geierslay.

of wine. It extends to the little Lieser River. The world-renowned name "Brauneberg" refers collectively to a large number of excellent sites;[95] on the opposite shore, Filzen, with Neufilzen, Brauneberg, and Mülheim; on the same side, a bit farther downstream, Lieser; all these localities share the Brauneberg hill. Brauneberg and Mülheim are home to a flourishing trade in wine.

The vicinity of Mülheim is interesting. On the right bank of the Mosel, Mülheim itself, which lies a bit inland, boasts the fine Elisenberg vineyard;[96] on the left bank, diagonally across, sits Lieser with the excellent Niederberg vineyard.[97] Small wine valleys converge from either side of the Mosel: to the right, the valley of the Veldenz crossed by the little stream Hinterbach, with the village of Veldenz alongside it; a bit farther back Burgen; to the left, the Lieser Valley with nearby villages Maring and Noviand, known for their red wine, and farther upstream, Osann and Platten. The vineyards downstream from Lieser, the village, run seamlessly into those of Andel and Kues. Kues also has a reputation as a center for wine commerce.

Bernkastel stands on the left flank of a marching column of first-rate vineyards that tightly pack the right bank of the Mosel all the way to Zeltingen. Just beyond the picturesque town of Bernkastel lies one of the best known and most renowned of the entire Mosel: the Doctor vineyard.[98] Who does not know the story about the Archbishop and Prince-Elector of Trier, Bohemund II (died 1367), who cured himself by drinking Doctor wine when he was seriously ill!

95. The old site names on the south-facing Brauneberg hillside include Hasenläufer, Kammer, Falkenberg, Juffer (much smaller than today's eponymous *Einzellage*), Mötschert, and Burgerslay. (Falkenberg, Juffer, Mötschert, and Burgerslay are in the *Einzellage* Brauneberger Juffer Sonnenuhr.)

96. Elisenberg is an estimable ca. 4-ha site facing south, with a fairly deep soil of gray slate and quartzite, further inland in a cool side valley and closer to Veldenz. The hillside is colored light red on Clotten's tax map. Max Ferd. Richter was then and still is well known for its Elisenberger wines. In 1815, the vineyard was planted by Franz Ludwig Niessen. This privileged land was given to him after he saved Mülheim and Veldenz from being sacked by Napoleon's army in 1813.

97. Niederberg, or Lieserer-Niederberg, is the prime south-facing hillside, now called Lieserer Niederberg-Helden. On the cadastral map, Helden is a place name in the central part of the slope.

98. The third letter of this site's name, like the fifth letter in its commune's name, fluctuates historically between "c" and "k," and although the word for doctor in German is *Doktor*, the current official vineyard name is "Doctor." Both Wwe. Dr. H. Thanisch estates (Erben Thanisch and Erben Müller-Burggraef) spell "Berncastel" with a "c" solely on the labels of their Doctor wine.

But the name "Doctor" did endure
for both the wine and hillside,
It still makes sick folk well today—
and healthy people happy!

Doctor wine must not only have cured Bohemund but also tasted good to him, since just before he stepped down, he managed to obtain from his successor a written authorization to take with him 20 *Fuder* from the Bernkastel diocesan cellars.

Above the town, in the vineyards, lies Landshut Castle; along the riverbank, the ancient administrative building, where the Trier archbishop's cellarmaster lived and the tithe wine was stored;[99] on the market square, the old town hall where three valuable goblets from the castle are on display.

Bernkastel is home to an important wine trade, a good viticultural school, and around 100 ha of vineyards, including the superior sites of Graben, Schwan, and Rosenberg.[100]

Situated across the river is the well-known Cusanus Hospital,[101] not actually a hospital, but, rather, a retirement home, where, according to its founding charter, 33 male beneficiaries find refuge. Near the hospital lies the station of the branch line that connects Bernkastel-Kues with the Koblenz–Trier railway.[102]

99. Built in the mid-17th century, the Ehemalige Kurfürstliche Amtskellerei (former cellars of the prince-elector) were confiscated by the French and then auctioned to the mayor of Bernkastel in 1803. Later, the facility was in the possession of the city parish until around the time Koch wrote this book, before being sold to the local government and turned into a school. Between 1971 and 2010, it housed the *Berufsschule für Weinbau*. Today, there are plans to transform the building into a hotel.

100. Rosenberg (not to be confused with the *Einzellage* Bernkastel-Kueser Rosenberg) is a former site nowadays split among the *Einzellagen*—Bernkasteler Matheisbildchen, Bratenhöfchen, and Lay, which were once much smaller sites too. The wines from Bratenhöfchen, Matheisbildchen, as well as the neighboring *Einzellagen* Bernkasteler Johannisbrünnchen and Graben, are usually labeled for the larger collective site, or *Grosslage*, "Bernkasteler Badstube," the smallest Mosel *Grosslage* with only 68 ha, thus smaller than many *Einzellagen*, and one of the very few *Grosslage* designations still routinely employed by reputable German producers. The original Badstube is the 1.6-ha *Einzellage* Alte Badstube am Doctorberg (*Gewann* In der Badstube), which abuts the famous 3.2-ha Doctor vineyard to the east.

101. This institution owes the name under which it is usually identified to that of its celebrated 15th-century founder Cardinal Nicholas of Cusa (Kues), known in Latin as Nicolaus Cusanus. The 33 male beneficiaries represented the lifespan of Jesus Christ. Today, the home serves approximately 60 men and women.

102. The connection Bernkastel-Kues to Wittlich ceased operations in 1989. Today, it is a

On the right bank, surrounded by vineyards, sits Graach, with many outstanding sites, such as Himmelreich[103] and Kirchenlay.[104] At the end of the village on the wine route that runs between the river and the vineyards lies Josephshof with its picturesque press house, once a property of the Trier monastery St. Martin and formerly known as Martinshof, a monastic property confiscated under French rule and sold to that praiseworthy champion of Mosel winegrowing Josef Hain. Since 1858, the property has belonged to Graf von Kesselstatt. The wine name Josephshöfer is known worldwide today.[105]

Next, along the left bank, comes Wehlen, its excellent vineyards situated on the opposite bank.[106] At the beginning of the 18th century, the wines in the Archdiocese of Trier were ranked in five classes, and among these only the wines of Wehlen were in the first class. In Wehlen, as in many Rheingau villages, a custom once prevailed known as *Weingabelung*, whereby wines were offered for sale in lots comprising both better and lesser sorts, for which a mid-price was agreed upon with the buyers.[107]

bicycle path.

103. At the time of the book's publication, Himmelreich (*Gewann* Im Himmelreich) designated only a small part of the current 62-ha *Einzellage* Graacher Himmelreich.

104. Kirchenlay (also spelled Kirchenlai, Kirchlay, or Kirchley) is an official named section, like the adjacent Domprobstbann, that is located on a steep slope above the village church within today's *Einzellage* Graacher Domprobst, although some of the best sites in Graach are actually located in the vastly expanded Graacher Himmelreich, such as Absberg, just up the slope from Josephshöfer, or the ur-Himmelreich itself.

105. The prime 5.7-ha Josephshöfer, located between Graacher Domprobst and Wehlener Sonnenuhr, is an *Alleinbesitz* (exclusive possession) of Reichsgraf von Kesselstatt. Its heavily weathered gray slate soil at the foot of the slope is relatively deep. Josephshöfer refers to both the low-lying Pichter vineyard on the riverbank and to the larger and better Münzlay sector on the slope.

106. Two of the top former sites within the nearly 43-ha *Einzellage* Wehlener Sonnenuhr (once only 8 ha) are Nonnenberg, close to Josephshöfer, and Lammerterlay, where a sundial was built by Jodocus Prüm in 1842. Today's 1.5-ha *Einzellage* Wehlener Nonnenberg is actually across the river from the slate slope on flat ground.

107. According to the historical account offered by Dr. Petri in Dr. Friedrich Wilhelm Dünkelberg's 1867 *Der Nassauische Weinbau* (best known today for its accompanying map classifying Rheingau vineyards, considered the earliest German example of its genre), *Weingabelung* arose as a means to ensure the sale of lesser wines as well as to ensure that buyers in more distant, less lucrative markets were offered quality wares. According to Petri, the last such *Weingabelung* in the Rheingau took place in 1726, by which time legislation stipulated that in the absence of *Weingabelung*, an official minimum price would be put into effect.

On the right bank is Zeltingen, which forms a joint municipality with Rachtig and is a very important winegrowing center with more than 175 ha. When it comes to quantity, this district stands at the top of the entire production area of the Mosel. Many a fine drop of wine comes from here as well, and Schlossberger has seized a place in the front row among the best Mosel wines.[108] Many wine merchants are based in Zeltingen.

The vineyards continue along the left bank into Ürzig, which possesses— albeit 3 km up the hill from the village—a train station on the Koblenz–Trier railway. A quite good vineyard site bears the odd name Krankenlay.[109] Situated on the right bank, Erden boasts excellent, terraced vineyards on the opposite left bank, among them Treppchen,[110] which, as the name indicates, can be reached only by steps. Lösenich is also on the right bank, with good vineyards on the left. The Mosel flows between Kinheim and its affiliated settlement Kindel, but the vineyards are situated on the left bank. At Kröv, on the left, and Wolf, on the right, wine is grown on both sides of the river, though the best sites lie on the left bank. Kröv also trades in wine.

At Wolf, the Traben Hill pushes the Mosel sideways, into a barely open oxbow, virtually entwining that entire ridge of hills. High up on the left bank are the ruins of the Mont Royal fortress, built by the French in 1686 under Louis XIV. This stronghold of the Mosel did not last long. Following the

108. Eduard Puricelli, a German industrialist and politician who built the impressive neo-Renaissance château in Lieser in 1895, sold his wines at auction in Trier. His daughter married the Prussian official Clemens Freiherr von Schorlemer in 1880, and in 1895 she inherited the property, which her husband later named "Schloss Lieser." The family owned top vineyards in Zeltingen (Schlossberg, aka Burg, Kakert, and Rotlay), Wehlen, Graach, Lieser, Brauneberg (Falkenberg or *Gewann* Im Falkenberg), Wintrich (Ohligsberg and Neuberg), and, later, in Serrig (Würtzberg). They received many royal visitors to their estate, including German Emperor Wilhelm II. In the 1890s, the Ehes-Berres and Franz Merrem estates also owned top parcels in Zeltingen, including Schlossberg, and auctioned their wines in Trier.

109. "Kranklay," which literally means the "sick people's slate," designates a prime spot at the foot of the post-1971 *Einzellage* Ürziger Würzgarten. The official *Gewann* on the cadastral map is named In der Kranklei. (On Clotten's 1868 and 1890 maps, the site is spelled "Kranklai.")

110. The original Erdener Treppchen (which includes Erdener Prälat or *Gewann* In Onnerts), just downstream from Kranklay, was only a small section of the steep hillside with "little steps." Today's 36.3-ha *Einzellage* Erdener Treppchen, with its red iron-rich slate soil, extends much farther downstream and includes, among others, the top sites Herzlay and Buslay (not to be confused with the 57.9-ha *Einzellage* Erdener Bußlay, which took its name and is on flat land).

1697 Peace of Ryswick, it was razed.[111] Beneath, at the edge of precipitous vineyard slopes, lies the ancient miniature village of Rissbach. From there, the Mosel shoots through a narrow ravine toward two localities, Trarbach and Traben, which, although separated by the river,[112] enjoy very active commercial intercourse. Trarbach lies on the right bank, wedged into a small side valley towered over by the picturesque, ruined Grevenburg; while Traben, with the additional space available to it, is further spread out along the left bank. Both villages have important vineyard sites, together more than 175 ha, including the excellent Schlossberg, Ungsberg, and Halsberg[113] in Trarbach, as well as Unterburg and Schimmelsberg in Traben. Some excellent red wine is grown in the Trabener Schlossberg. These two communities represent one of the most remarkable places in the whole Mosel area because of their winegrowing, but even more because of their exceptionally active commerce in wine. Wholesale trade, in particular, is based in Traben-Trarbach and, through this market hub, whose vast cellars primarily accommodate wine from the Middle Mosel, many thousand *Fuder* are shipped annually to the whole world.[114]

Incidentally, in the Trarbach Casino, known for its excellent wine list, a party was thrown one night in the autumn of 1845 following the first German-Flemish song festival for choral societies from Koblenz to Trier. As people became vividly aware of the absence of any Mosel song, Dr. Graff from Trarbach offered as a toast these auspicious words: "Whoever writes a Mosel song like the one that Matthias Claudius [1740–1815] wrote about the Rhine—'On the Rhine, On the Rhine, there grow our vines'—will win

111. Mont Royal, part of a defense line along France's northern frontier, was built by Louis XIV's chief military engineer Sébastien le Prestre de Vauban (1633–1707), like the fortifications of the town of Trarbach and those of many other cities, such as Luxembourg and Saarlouis.

112. The first bridge was inaugurated just a couple of years after Koch's visit and was built by the Berlin architect Bruno Möhring, who later built many of the Jugendstil buildings in Traben-Trarbach, such as the hotel and wine shop Clauss-Feist, now named Jugendstilhotel Bellevue. He was also responsible for the pavilion and restaurant of German wine producers at the 1900 Paris Exhibition.

113. After 1971, Halsberg became subsumed into an *Einzellage* bearing the once celebrated name "Trarbacher Schlossberg," a site made famous by A. Böcking. Farther up the secluded side valley of Kautenbach are the top sites of Ungsberg and Hühnerberg.

114. In the 1890s, the collective cavernous cellars of Traben-Trarbach's numerous wine merchants could accommodate 15,000 *Fuder*.

a *Fuder* of the best Mosel wine." The following spring, the Trarbach Casino earned a lasting reputation for organizing a contest for the best folk song about Mosel wine, with a *Fuder* of the best quality as the prize. Poetic gold rewarded with the liquid gold of the Mosel! One can read about the flood of songs that were spilled out across the Mosel region in those days in Dr. Josef Blumberger's small book *Moselwein und Mosellied* (Mosel Wine and Mosel Song, 1886). More than 200 songs were entered in the competition, but there was much chaff among the wheat, and since the mistake had been made to appoint only musicians on the jury, the prize was awarded, as Blumberger puts it, to "a hymn, well-crafted and enthusiastically rousing, but not remotely suited by text or melody to become part of the public domain."

That song is forgotten today! But there was also a pearl among them, at least text-wise: the wonderful Mosel song by Theodor Reck, "Through the wide German land run many streams," whose melody the genius of Georg Schmitt conceived several years later, so that it soon conquered the people's hearts along the entire Mosel. And yet, it is not really what was wanted— namely, "A folk song about Mosel wine." Is it really possible to conjure up something like that through a competition? Must it not grow spontaneously and unconstrained, like the wild roses of the Mosel Valley? It will yet come![115]

The towns of Trarbach and Traben have shared the cruel fate of being devastated by fire. They are therefore predominantly modern in character.[116] On the Traben side is the terminal of the secondary rail line, which connects the town with the Koblenz–Trier railway at Bullay.

Beyond Traben comes the adjoining fishing village of Litzig, and, on the heights to the right, the hamlet of Starkenburg, from whence a vine-clad, mountain-like face stretches to Enkirch, whose houses clamber up onto the slope, and whose vineyard area of more than 125 ha is one of the largest on the Mosel.

115. Ernst Julius Otto, a cantor from Dresden, won the contest with his song "Des Deutschen Rheines Braut" (The Bride of the German Rhine). "Mosellied" (Mosel Song) earned second place. Theodor Reck (1815–1873), who wrote the lyrics for "Mosellied"—which figures throughout Koch's text—was a Protestant parish priest in Feldkirchen on the Rhine. Georg Schmitt (1821–1900), born in Trier, was the cantor of Saint-Sulpice and Saint-Germain-des-Prés in Paris.

116. The fire swept through the right-bank town of Trarbach on July 21, 1857. About 1,400 of 1,700 inhabitants lost their homes. From today's perspective, it is "modern" Jugendstil architecture that gives Traben and Trarbach their distinctive touristic charm.

Good sites include Steffensberg,[117] Hinterberg,[118] and Monteneubel. From Enkirch came the wine that the casino in Trarbach gave as a prize at the song competition. It was a precious *Fuder* of 1846 *Jungfernwein*[119] from the newly established Batterieberg vineyard.[120] Opposite Enkirch lies the picturesque village of Kövenich, which has a railway station on the branch line mentioned above. Kövenich has a magnificent view of the vineyards of Enkirch across the Mosel River.

Enkirch concludes the succession of Middle Mosel communities in which its principal wines are produced. To be sure, winegrowing remains important in the entire valley, and, in the steep, often terraced vineyards, a product is achieved that, although not laying claim to a place in the top echelon, nevertheless contributes to the renown of Mosel wine. It is precisely an advantage of the Mosel's production that it offers its racy wine not just for those with deep pockets but also those with modest budgets. The following villages remain to be mentioned: Burg, Reil, Pünderich, Briedel, Kaimt, Zell, Merl, Bullay, Alf, St. Aldegund, Neef, Bremm, Eller, Ediger, Nehren, Senheim, Senhals, Mesenich, Briedern, Poltersdorf, Beilstein, Ellenz, Fankel, Bruttig, Ernst, Valwig, and Sehl. Trading in wine is carried out in Enkirch, Pünderich, Zell, Merl, St. Aldegund, Ediger, Ellenz, Beilstein, and Bruttig.[121]

117. Steffensberg (also spelled Stephansberg), much like Dhroner Hofberg, was a renowned right-bank side-valley vineyard in Koch's day. A choice part of the south-facing slope is a specific site called Löwenbaum (*Gewann* Im Löwenbaum), marked dark red on Markworth's tax map.

118. Hinterberg includes such top sites, on terraces, as Zeppwingert, Batterieberg, and Ellergrub.

119. The maiden wine bottled from a newly planted vineyard, usually in the second or third year after planting.

120. The nickname "battery," which has stuck to this vineyard *monopole*, alludes to its having been blasted out of the hillside, starting in 1841, by owner and demolitions expert Carl August Immich, by no means the sole occasion when such measures were taken to improve a Mosel site's exposure or quantity of pulverized slate. (The prize winner actually received 300 liters from a *Fuder* of 1846 Batterieberg.)

121. Koch's relative disregard for sites downstream from Enkirch is not entirely consistent with the contemporary record. (He was not the only contemporary commentator to have neglected them.) Markworth's tax map of the Lower Mosel for the district of Koblenz, first published in the same year (1897) as Koch's Mosel book, shows a number of villages with highly rated sites colored dark red, including Winningen, Kobern, Hatzenport, Gondorf, Merl, Valwig, Fankel, and Ellenz-Poltersdorf. The success of the Trier auctions for Saar and Mosel wines led winegrowers from the Lower Mosel and Middle Rhine to auction their wines in Koblenz in the hall of the Görresbau.

The area under vine between Piesport and Cochem includes about 3,200 ha, which produces, on average, about 9,000 *Fuder* a year—i.e., more than half of the total production on the Middle and Lower Mosel.

The Mosel from Cochem to Koblenz

Between Cochem and Klotten, the Mosel makes yet another sharp bend,[122] thereafter concluding in smoother meanders along the final stretch of its course to Koblenz. The steep riverbanks on the right face mostly northeast and on the left bank southwest. Only near Cochem and along the short stretch between Kobern and Winningen does the Mosel flow in such a way that the main expanse of vineyards faces south. As a result of the more favorable sun exposure of these sites, along the Lower Mosel the three communities of Cochem, Kobern, and Winningen most notably excel in the production of superior wine.

In the remaining villages, terraced vineyards, artfully laid out and impeccably tended, yield mostly average-quality wine, though it is always distinguished by good *Gähre*[123] and genuine Mosel character. One gazes with astonishment at the narrow vine rows, which the vintner has with tireless diligence, unshakable perseverance, and unspeakable effort wrested, one meager piece at a time, from often barely accessible cliffs.

122. The final sharp bend that completes the long series of oxbows is known as Cochemer Krampen. The course of the Mosel between Bremm and Cochem is shaped like a cramp (or clamp), hence the name. The Kaiser-Wilhelm-Tunnel (also known as Cochemer Tunnel), built between 1874 and 1877 to link Ediger-Eller and Cochem, bypasses Krampen and was once the longest railroad tunnel in Germany.

123. An indeterminate approbative wine buzzword of the time (also spelled *Gör, Göhr, Gahre, Göhre, Gäre,* etc.), whose survival into the 20th century is probably due, in part, precisely to its ambiguity and elasticity. Given that *gären* means "to ferment," the term suggests possible allusion to felicitous completion of fermentation, or perhaps to vivacity from dissolved CO_2 (a cardinal Mosel wine virtue of Koch's time). Baedeker's 1895 *Rheinlande,* comparing Saar wine with Mosel, alleges the former's "*grössere Gäre,*" which it parenthetically defines (with rare explicitness) as "greater amount of CO_2." In some contexts, pleasing astringency or aromatic intensity seem possible connotations. The Grimm brothers' mid-19th-century dictionary cites those last two usages but also alleges the English expression "good garb" as a cognate. Wine literature of Koch's era sometimes suggests *Gähre* as a translation of the equally indeterminate French *sève.* The more familiar *Rasse,* or "race," is a similarly broad, amorphous approbation that can nonetheless, in some contexts, suggest wine possessing lively acidity or spiciness. The adjective form is *göhrig* or *görig.*

Here is that stretch of the Mosel Valley where fairytale romanticism reaches its greatest splendor. In the narrow gorge, the villages cling to the sheer wall of the hillside; the old houses, witnesses to a long-forgotten era, are shoved hither and thither, with picturesque castle walls towering above. Here is the Mosel's so-called Valley of the Knights, where in a nine-hour stretch you will sail beneath the gaze of no fewer than 12 castles.

Cochem is considered a highlight of the Mosel. On the bend at the hamlet of Sehl, a vista opens to the renowned view of Cochem, where one's attention is captured, above all, by the former Imperial Reichsburg that rises above the town atop steep cliffs. It is a magnificently evocative picture: high up, the castle, newly expanded in genuinely medieval style, not in mere fantasy style, with the jagged, pitched roofs of its many towers; then, below against the cliffs, the old Mosel town, scarcely less sharply angular than the castle above.[124] Behind the town, Winneburg ruin rises out of the savagely romantic Ender Valley, and on the opposite bank of the Mosel lies the hamlet of Cond.

The area under vines at Cochem and Cond is more than 100 ha, and the production from some good sites is nowadays counted among the Mosel's better wines. A lively wine trade flourishes in both localities. At Cochem begins the big tunnel—Germany's most significant at 4.2 km long—that conducts the Koblenz–Trier railway upstream. From Cochem downstream, the railway runs directly along the river almost the entire way to Koblenz.

Winegrowing continues in steep, rocky, arduous-to-cultivate sites downstream to Klotten and Pommern, which together possess somewhere between 150 and 175 ha of vineyards. In Klotten, there is also commerce in wine. Then follows Treis with approximately 45 ha and diagonally across from it, Karden. There is a somber grandeur to the landscape, out of which solemnly gazes Karden, with its ancient St. Castor's Church and the picturesque, fortified medieval *Burghaus* of the prince-elector's chosen local magistrate. Between Müden and Moselkern, on the right, runs the

---

124. Jacob Louis Frédric Ravené, an iron and steel wholesaler from Berlin, bought the castle from the Prussian state in 1868 and hired architects to have it reconstructed in the 1870s for use as a summer residence. Today, it is a museum owned by the city of Cochem. Ravené initially wanted to purchase Grevenburg in Traben-Trarbach, but the winegrowers didn't want to give up their vineyards that were close to the castle ruins.

narrow Lütz Valley, in which at Lütz itself vines are still planted, and, to the left, the wild Eltz Valley, with the completely preserved medieval Burg Eltz. Every part of it is original. It is a real landmark of the Mosel. By way of Burgen, one comes to Hatzenport, where, amid terraced vineyards, the ruins of the Bischofstein Castle quite magnificently adorn the steep hillside. Hatzenport has more than 50 ha of vineyards, including the fine site known as Tafelgutberg.[125] Next come Brodenbach, Löf, and Alken with the hoary, dilapidated walls of the double-towered Thurant Castle, which, in the 13th century, resisted a siege so long that the besieging troops allegedly drank 3,000 *Fuder* of wine. Past Kattenes, Oberfell, Moselsürsch, Lehmen (known for its production of red wine), Kühr, Niederfell, and Gondorf, the Mosel flows on to Kobern, Dieblich, and Winningen, where winegrowing, once again, achieves fine heights in terms of quality as well as quantity. Kobern has about 45 ha of vineyards, and Winningen no fewer than some 155 ha, but only a few vineyards belong to Dieblich. Especially famous is the Uhlen vineyard, its countless terraces built into the sheer rock face along the Mosel's left bank, between Kobern and Winningen.[126] Also of special note at Kobern are the Fahrberg and Rosenberg[127] vineyards, and, at Winningen, downstream from the village, the Röttgen vineyard, packed to the limit with vines. There is also a trade in wine at Winningen.

The convivial old custom of bringing the harvest to a close with a vintage festival has gradually declined along the Mosel. Only in Winningen have remnants of it been maintained, although nowadays young men celebrate the *Winzerfest* in black jackets and top hat and the girls in white dresses. This amounts to the poetry of winegrowing as gala. But at the festival dinner they eat only off of pewter tableware, and the good old days are thereby affirmed.

Lay, Güls, and Moselweiss are the last villages along the Lower Mosel, where the vines reflect in the shimmering river. Their numbers are no

125. Tafelgutberg is part of the present-day *Einzellage* Hatzenporter Stolzenberg, which comprises the *Gewanne* Im Tafelgut and Im Stolzenberg.

126. Uhlen belongs to both communities. Since 1971, producers can choose which village to designate on their labels.

127. Rosenberg is a site in the post-1971 *Einzellage* Koberner Weissenberg. Fahrberg today designates a separate *Einzellage* located between Weissenberg and Uhlen.

longer very large. The poetry of viticulture on the Mosel comes to an end with the delightful legend of *"Miseräbelchen"* ("the little miserable one"), which Karl Simrock (1802–1876) places in Güls in his *Rhine Legends* (1836). The little tumblers typically used for serving wine on the Lower Mosel are famously known as *"Miseräbelchen"* and that name will doubtless remain with them for all eternity.

Along the route from Cochem to Koblenz, around 925 ha serve for winegrowing, and the average crop might amount to about 2,700 *Fuder*, or slightly less than a fifth of the total wine harvest of the Middle and Lower Mosel.

There are no Mosel vineyards in the immediate vicinity of Koblenz. Nevertheless, Koblenz—at the terminus of the production area for Mosel wine—has evolved every bit as intimately with that wine as has Trier at the region's gateway. Even though it is known as *"Koblenz am Rhein,"* Koblenz is and will remain a genuine Mosel city.

On its Mosel side, Koblenz has preserved its old medieval face; but not on the Rhine side, to which the city has since expanded. There is no doubt that city life was more active on the Mosel in earlier centuries. The still-standing Mosel Bridge, built in 1344, connected Koblenz with the bustling Lützel-Koblenz until, among other blows of fate suffered by Lützel, in 1688, amid the distress of war, it was completely shot to pieces. Fourteen years later, what remained of Lützel-Koblenz merged with Neuendorf. The bridge was, over the years, the scene of some peculiar customs. On New Year's Day, the venerable town council consumed a small Dutch cheese, a couple of capons, a cake, and a quarter-boiled egg on the bridge; on Walpurgis Night (April 30), both mayors strolled back and forth on it and handed out flowers to every woman they came across, young and old; and at fairs, youngsters were allowed to dance on the bridge until nightfall. At the bridge, opposite the old castle, the noble citizens put on helmets and armor on the archbishop's name day, in order to receive a complimentary drink from three *Fuder* of wine.

The well-preserved Archbishop's Castle at the Mosel Bridge was built in 1276, not without bad blood from the citizens of Koblenz, who did not want such a hulk within the city walls.

The prince-electors often stayed in the castle. Many jugs filled with good Mosel wine may have shared the fate of all wines when the electors stayed there! During French rule, the castle's grandeur came to an end.[128] It was sold and demoted to a factory for varnished metal sheets. The city of Koblenz put an end to this condition in 1896. It bought the remarkable ancient building and plans to maintain and use it in a dignified manner.[129]

Koblenz is a very important center for the wine trade,[130] and the fact that Mosel wine plays a leading role in this trade is hardly a surprise to anyone who knows what a fine appreciation there is in this city for the racy produce of the Mosel. Koblenz is proud of its Mosel wines.

At Koblenz, the Rhine sends the Mosel off into the wide, wide world. It is not granted to its waters to remain at home, and as often as those waters renew themselves, they must eternally wander forth from their homeland. It is no different with its wines. As often as the sunbeams hit against the slate walls and ripen the grapes, the wine must get out into the wide, wide world. There is only one Mosel wine. Where else can all the thirsty souls get Mosel wine than from the Mosel!

128. In 1786, the last prince-elector of Trier, the maternal uncle of Louis XVI, moved the capital to Koblenz. After the French Revolution, the brothers of Louis XVI and other French émigrés resided there for several years until the invasion of French Republican troops.

129. Renovation work on the Old Castle, *Alte Burg*, was taking place as Koch wrote. Today, the castle holds the city archives.

130. The famous wine merchant and sparkling-wine producer Deinhard & Co., which was based in Koblenz, employed 164 workers and owned an estate in Rüdesheim-Oestrich in the Rheingau. Deinhard acquired an estate in Bernkastel with holdings in the famous Doctor vineyard in 1900. Julius Wegeler, who was the manager of Deinhard and president of the German Winegrowers' Association, had a gravity-flow press house and cellar built in Kues in 1903.

Ravages to Riches: Mosel Wine's Long Nineteenth Century

by Kevin Goldberg, Ph.D.

Karl Heinrich Koch's poetic, late-19th-century snapshot of Mosel wine strikes a familiar chord with contemporary wine lovers. His verse resonates with charm and grace, and his portrayals of Mosel vineyards and wines conjure the kind of beauty and cheer familiar to those who visit the region today. To quote Koch, Mosel wine "tantalizes." However, the interval between Koch's golden 1890s and our own epoch has hardly been one of steady success for the Mosel. Like history in general, the trade has been marked more by zigs and zags, booms and busts, than by slow and certain improvement in wine quality, reputation, and prices paid. In fact, in 1926, a mere generation after the publication of Koch's masterpiece, 2,000 vintners and wine traders stormed through the very heart of the *Mittelmosel*, plundering and burning Bernkastel's tax and revenue office, demanding assistance from the state. From the heights of the Mosel trade in the 1890s to its near collapse in the 1920s—due largely to the repercussions of Germany's stinging defeat in the First World War—history's volatility becomes strikingly clear.

In the grandiose tenor of his words and his exalted ideas, Koch doesn't exaggerate at all the wonderfulness of the wines. The 1890s was, by many accounts, a boom decade for the Mosel trade, like nothing before or since. While success in the wine trade is never spread evenly across social classes, in the 1890s many vintners and merchants benefited from the upward spiral of wine quality, reputation, and price. Barren and mixed-use land, especially south-facing slate slopes in the side valleys of the Saar and Ruwer, were converted to viticulture by growers, merchants, and the state, often with the intention of capitalizing on the region's renown, as well as establishing test vineyards, schools, and vinicultural labs to improve wine quality. Domestically and even abroad, *Moselwein* flatteringly came to be called *Modewein* ("fashionable wine"). No greater compliment could be given to the region as a whole than the increasingly common assertion in the wine press that the Mosel had surpassed the legendary Rheingau as the source of Germany's best wines.

Those on the Mosel who were then old enough to remember the 1840s, the so-called Hunger Decade, would have been astonished by the region's turnaround, which began in earnest in the 1860s. Although the Mosel's golden age from the 1880s to the 1920s was determined largely by external political, social, and economic factors, that did not mean that Mosel growers and merchants lazily benefited as their landholdings skyrocketed in value, and their auctioned wines fetched record prices. The innate advantages offered by nature were part of a bigger picture, which includes industrious growers, the use of appropriate technologies and sales strategies, and an understanding of consumer tastes. Fully unpacking the reasons for the Mosel's upswing requires a brief excursion into the dynamics of state and society.

Unlike most of Europe, Germany was a latecomer to nation status. Created from a collection of states, duchies, and free cities, the German Empire entered onto the world stage only in 1871. Among the dozens of territories, Prussia had been the dominant military and economic force, and it was on Prussia's terms that Germany was born. The Mosel Valley, a historically Catholic area with a discernible Franco-Liberal streak, had been paradoxically incorporated into Protestant and militaristic Prussia following Napoleon's defeat. In many ways, the late-century success of the Mosel wine trade hinged on Prussia's rising-star status within German and European power politics.

The unification of Germany coincided with its industrialization and with the commercialization of German society. Though the towns and villages along the Mosel were not themselves transformed into industrial centers, the impact on the region was significant. As Koch points out, the first Trier–Koblenz rail line was completed in 1879, opening the river valley to cargo and—more important—to tourists. In addition, the construction of roads and bridges and the rising standard of living were boons for many domestic industries, including wine. From the Bavarian Alps to the Baltic Coast, luxury hotels and restaurants eager to offer the finest German wines sprang up seemingly overnight. The German middle class was nationalist to the core and had become a voracious consumer of German wine. Driving this market toward the Mosel, above all other German wine regions, required the courage, ingenuity, and know-how of the region's growers and merchants.

By the 1890s, winegrowing had become bureaucratized and made into a scientific and rational discipline. Instead of exclusively learning the trade through kin, as had until then prevailed, vintners in the 1890s were benefiting from schools and reaping the fruits of enological research, including from abroad. Even poor and part-time vintners profited from these same advances through instructional books or the educational efforts of the many cooperatives that had proliferated since the 1850s. This was essential for growers whose vineyard parcels had dwindled in size due to the region's partible inheritance laws under which landholdings were generally divided among children with each new generation. While centuries-old family knowledge still may have held a few secrets, there was no putting a stop to the professionalization of winegrowing and its technological and administrative modernization at the turn of the last century.

In a similar vein, the merchant side of the trade had thoroughly revolutionized in the wake of German unification and industrialization. Vertical integration had increased efficiency and now capital was available for both necessary and experimental purchases. Several firms targeted product or market niches. For example, Mosel wine firms that specialized in exporting to Britain did particularly well in the 1890s, all the more effectively with the increased use of glass bottles and corks. Generally, the firms that succeeded best were those able to combine historical trade networks with modern sales strategies. Some others had inside political information about trade agreements or tax and tariff policy, or they had special access to government and other large contracts.

A signature feature of the 1890s Mosel wine boom was the wine auction. Though a number of independent families and cooperatives hosted their own auctions, none was more successful than the annual festivities held in Trier. Koch gives us a contemporary sense for the excitement and thrill (and astounding prices!) of these occasions. Many of the same villages and vineyards celebrated today became fabled sources for the world's greatest wines at these auctions: Piesporter, Scharzhofberger, Brauneberger, and Bernkasteler Doctor, to name a few. Though wine auctions existed well before the 1890s, they took on a special significance in the waning decades of the 19th century as clever producers learned to market and distribute more efficiently. By pooling their resources to form larger auctions, producers were able to cut costs and offer buyers greater convenience. Besides, these pre-War auctions featured a style of wine that was *not* decidedly sweet like those typically under hammer at today's Grosser Ring and Bernkasteler Ring auctions.

The great majority of auctions, especially those on the Mosel, were exclusively involved with the sale of so-called natural wine (as today, the words had no hard-and-fast definition). Natural wine in the 1890s generally referred to wine that originated from musts to which neither sugar nor water had been added. Top producers at these Trier auctions, usually held in the spring, sold most of their wines in traditional 1,000-liter *Fuder* casks. Other traditions, however, were swept away in the wash of rapid change that marked the late 19th century. One of the by-products of industrialization was the technologization of food-and-drink production, which sparked fears (justified or not) among traditional growers. The so-called *Kunstweinfrage* (artificial-wine question) wracked the German wine trade in the latter half of the 19th century. Tensions were aggravated by self-described purists who abstained from manipulating wine through processes such as de-acidification and chaptalization (both fairly common in the global wine trade today). The Mosel was a key battleground in the natural vs. artificial debates, and it would take decades for the Mosel as a whole to shake off its reputation as a region for "artificial" wines. Auctions were the driving force in challenging this reputation.

Of course, many of the changes described above affected other German wine regions (the Rheingau, Rheinhessen, the Pfalz) just as they had the Mosel. What then, specifically, accounts for the Mosel's surge to the top of the wine world in the 1890s? Those who have had direct encounters with the wine and area know the answer best. As Koch notes, despite the great divergences in price and quality up and down the river and its side valleys, there is still an inexplicable, yet somehow tangible *Moselrasse* (Mosel breed) evident in the region's wine. As it did for Koch, Mosel wine continues to tantalize the intellects and palates of wine drinkers with its freshness and its ability to make the vineyards speak through the wines. Still more, the Mosel and its two most important tributaries—the Saar and Ruwer—were and remain blanketed on both banks by lush forests, spectacularly preserved villages, awe-inspiring castle ruins, and most important of all, rows and rows of verdant Riesling vineyards, many of which were initially planted in the 19th century. At some locations, the steep hillside cliffs and craggy terraces look too daunting for the delicate handwork necessary to cultivate healthy vines, but this is partly how the wines achieve their magnificence. The second half of the 19th century made manifest what had been latent in the almost 2,000 years of viticulture that went before: the Mosel's unique ability to produce some of the world's greatest wine. ◆

This essay is adapted from "Mosel Wine: Light, Zappy, and Dry" in The Art of Eating, *issue no. 96, which was the first part of a three-part article published in May 2016 and revised in March 2019 (see www.artofeating.com/issue-no-96/).*

The Heyday of Mosel Wine in the 1890s

by Lars Carlberg

Popular wisdom has it that all German Riesling, especially from the much-loved Mosel Valley, is sweet. Although this false perception has diminished in recent years, old beliefs are hard to shake. The most ardent fans and even many producers of Mosel Riesling are probably unaware that in the late 19th century, the region's heyday, most of the wines were dry and consumed fairly young. While there has long been a tradition of making age-worthy, sweet Auslese wines from ripe grapes, usually affected by the botrytis fungus, or "noble rot" (which shrivels the grapes, concentrating their sugars and acids), it turns out that the catapulting of Mosel wine onto the world stage was due largely to its charming youth. The great Mosel wines around 1900 were—much to our surprise today—light, zappy, and dry.

In September 1898, a 34-year-old Austrian chemist named Maximilian Ripper visited Trier to attend the 17th annual wine congress of the Deutscher Weinbau-Verein, a German winegrowers' association. Ripper came away impressed by the large turnout and the buzz surrounding Mosel wine, and he wrote an enthusiastic 19-page report titled *Moselweinbau und Moselwein* (Mosel Winegrowing and Mosel Wine, *Die Weinlaube*, Klosterneuburg), an essential eyewitness account from a neutral outsider.

Ripper explains that the five-day congress, which celebrated the association's 25th anniversary and drew many more visitors than expected, comprised various events, conferences, and tours. The topics included phylloxera, oidium (powdery mildew), peronospora (downy mildew), vine moths, and even "pure yeasts" (isolated cultured yeast strains). But the big draw was the tasting of over 100 Mosel wines from four recent vintages, including the great 1893 (very ripe), 1895, and 1897, as well as the lesser 1896.

Mosel wine had become a *Modewein*—a "fashionable wine"—after a difficult period from about 1827 to 1857, during which many vintages lacked ripeness and the winegrowers were heavily taxed and faced greater competition as the Prussian trading zone—officially known as the *Zollverein*, or German Customs Union—nearly monopolized by the Mosel since the 1815 annexation of the Rhineland, grew to include almost all German wine regions. In 1842, Karl Marx, who was born in Trier and whose family owned vines in the Viertelsberg sector of today's Maximin Grünhäuser Herrenberg vineyard, wrote in the *Rheinische Zeitung* about the hardships facing Mosel peasant growers—which prompted some to emigrate to America. The 1860s, however, marked the beginning of a new era that reached its zenith in the 1890s, which were the boom years of Mosel Riesling. Among the famous wines, most of them still famous today, were Scharzhofberger, Bocksteiner, Geisberger (all in the Saar subregion, the last now, finally, replanted), Piesporter, Brauneberger, and Zeltinger Schlossberger. (The renowned Schlossberg vineyard was back then the area around the ruins of the castle, or *Burg,* within the present Zeltinger Sonnenuhr.)

Mosel wines garnered a lot of attention in the German Empire and beyond. On wine lists at top restaurants and luxury hotels in Berlin, London, and New York, the best Mosels commanded higher prices than many of the finest Bordeaux, Burgundies, and Champagnes. These high-quality Mosel Rieslings, sometimes referred to as *Hochgewächse*, or "exalted growths," had been made famous by the Trier wine auctions, which were held each spring and brought the various estate owners, merchants, commissioners, and buyers under one roof. And after 1879 a new rail line between Trier and Koblenz made the wines more accessible than when they could only leave the region by steamboat or by the 1860 rail line between Trier and Saarbrücken. On the last day of the 1898 wine congress, the organizers had to cancel an excursion by steamboat down the Mosel from Trier to Traben-Trarbach because of low water; they took the train instead. (Until locks were built in the 1960s, the river wasn't navigable year-round; casks often had to be transported by oxcart.)

In March and April, wine buyers flocked to Trier to attend the auctions, where Mosel wine from the best sites was sold by the *Fuder* (the traditional oak cask of the Mosel, holding nearly 1,000 liters). These weren't merely limited quantities of a few chosen sweet Rieslings, such as those that dominate today's September (or November) auctions by the Grosser Ring, the Mosel-Saar-Ruwer regional association of the Verband Deutscher Prädikatsweingüter, or VDP. At the famous 1895 and 1896 Trier wine auctions, over 1,500 *Fuder* casks of the 1893 vintage were sold, the equivalent of almost 2 million bottles—which was still only about one-tenth of the total production in the Mosel wine region. For instance, Egon Müller auctioned 8 *Fuder* of 1893 Scharzberger and 28 *Fuder* of 1893 Scharzhofberger, or the equivalent of 48,000 bottles.

In the late 19th century, Mosel wines were specifically made to keep the pure Riesling aromas and a fresh, light prickle from residual carbon dioxide. They were consumed in their youth, unlike the renowned, longer-lived sweet Rhine wines, such as the coveted Auslesen from the Rheingau, Rheinhessen (Roter Hang), and the Pfalz (Mittelhaardt), which were often made from botrytised grapes. Mosels, with their pure Riesling scent and piquancy, represented the zeitgeist of modern industrial Germany with its faster tempo and newly affluent consumers. This period also saw the beginning of Jugendstil ("young style"), or Art Nouveau, in Germany, influencing many buildings in the Mosel Valley, for instance in the wine hub of Traben-Trarbach, as well as some of the most distinctive wine labels, such as Maximin Grünhaus and Immich-Batterieberg, then known as C. Aug. Immich. Ripper writes that German wine drinkers spent more money on top-quality wines than did his fellow Austrians. (Today, it's probably the other way around.) The famous sweet, golden Rhine wines were considered old-fashioned. (In those days, "sweet" probably implied no more than 30 grams of sugar per liter.) Ripper even wonders whether other German wine regions were seeking to imitate the vivacious dry-tasting wines of the Mosel. Now the opposite is true: the Mosel is better known for sweet wines, and the Rhine for dry.

Many of the best Rieslings in Germany are grown on slate hillsides, which, along with a cool climate, gives Mosel wine an inimitable imprint, in particular a floral, herbal perfume, a salty flavor, and a tangy acidity. The scientific explanations remain a mystery. "The best soil is slate mixed with quartz," wrote Franz Schneider in the Trier wine weekly *Der Winzer* in the issue of July 19, 1896. He said that it's important to have "a free, open, sunny site around morning and midday on the slope of a moderate hill." It's also good that a site be in an open valley, so the fog is "chased away." Schneider highlights the Saar for its predominantly rich, dry gray-clayey slate soils and flowery, spicy wines. He adds that the best soils—as in Oberemmel, Scharzberg, Wiltingen, Kanzem, and Bockstein—include "Wackenschiefer, so-called Beinling, a hard reddish-gray stone, usually mixed in with slate and intermingled deep down with a light-green, marl-like, fertile clayey earth." (Today, Saar growers often call this hard, reddish-gray, quartzite-bearing sandstone *Beinerling* or *Grauwacke*. But true graywacke, which doesn't exist in the Lower Mosel either, is granular and has a high amount of feldspars.) Red wine, from Pinot Noir, such as the once famous wines of Schabberg and Nonnenberg at Könen on the Saar, played only a minor role in the region, unlike farther north on the Ahr. Ripper notes that the traditional white wines made from Elbling grapes in the Upper Mosel, planted on calcareous soil and used mostly for sparkling wine, tended to be sour and without much aroma, though there were (and are) producers of high-quality Elbling (also known as Kleinberger). For centuries, this variety dominated much of the Mosel Valley, until growers in the Middle and Lower Mosel began to replace it with Riesling.

The Mosel, with its maritime coolness, is the most westerly rather than the most northerly German wine region. Ripper, who quoted Karl Heinrich Koch, says that a distinction was made, as today, between the Middle and Lower Mosel. He further divided the Middle Mosel in three: the lower reaches of the Saar; the Mosel from the mouth of the Saar to Piesport, including the vineyards of Trier and Ruwer; and the Mosel from Piesport to Cochem (though the border between the Middle and Lower Mosel wasn't clearly defined). Today, the Middle Mosel is considered to run roughly from Schweich, just downriver of Trier, to Pünderich and doesn't include the Ruwer, much less the Saar. (In 1909, the Middle Mosel was officially defined as being from Schweich to Traben-Trarbach and the Lower Mosel from Enkirch to Koblenz.) Ripper asserts that in the Middle Mosel the quantity and quality of the wines is far greater than in the Lower Mosel, where the river straightens out more (after Cochem). The Lower Mosel, also known today as the Terrassenmosel, boasted then as now some celebrated wines, such as in Winningen, with its dramatically steep, terraced vineyards, notably Uhlen and Röttgen.

In contrast to the calcareous Upper Mosel, as well as the vineyards of Luxembourg on the opposite bank, the Middle Mosel consists primarily of lime-free clayey gray and blue slate from the Devonian Period, though there are pockets with red slate as well. In Ürzig, the underlying red soil (Rotliegendes) includes sandstone (also in the Augenscheiner vineyard in Trier), while the steep slope facing the river has red slate and rhyolite, a volcanic stone unique among Mosel vineyards to Ürziger Würzgarten. The Lower Mosel features slate and, in parts, more quartzite, sandstone, and silt. The wines from warm sites, as in Winningen, tend to be riper and lower in acidity.

Until the Mosel-Saar-Ruwer region was legally established in 1909, all the wine was called simply *Moselwein,* though, as today, the Saar was often mentioned as a distinct subregion. "Mosel-Saar-Ruwer" was officially required on labels from 1936 to 2006, when for marketing reasons it was officially shortened to "Mosel"—an unpopular move among most Saar and Ruwer growers, who have since been permitted to indicate "Saar" and "Ruwer" on their labels.

The Saar flows into the Mosel just above Trier and the Ruwer below it. Ruwer and other side-valley wines, particularly around Trier on south-facing slopes in Avelsbach and Olewig, used to be called *Heckenweine,* "hedge wines." The hedges were made of *Lohhecke,* coppiced oak. The bark had been used by the thriving local leather-tanning industry, but during the height of Mosel wine, as the price of oak bark fell and the price of vineyard land dramatically rose, the shrubs and trees were cleared for vineyards, especially on privileged south-facing slopes in side valleys, such as at Geisberg in Ockfen (Saar) and at Kohlenberg, now known as Dominikanerberg, in Kasel (Ruwer). The Mosel had so many first-class vineyard sites, plus potentially great sites covered in *Lohhecken.* One of the very first maps of vineyards anywhere and a pioneering work in statistical cartography was the Royal Tax Assessor Franz Josef Clotten's 1868 *Saar und Mosel Weinbau-Karte* (Viticultural Map of the Saar and Mosel). Its color-coding based on tax assessments of vineyard land in the administrative district of Trier was used for marketing Saar and Mosel wines. The fourth and final 1906 edition shows all the new plantings.

On the third day of the 1898 congress, Ripper and a group of visitors took the train to the Saar and visited the Royal Prussian State Domain's newly established model winery in Ockfen in the Heppenstein, Oberherrenberg, and Bockstein vineyards (all three in the upper part of the present-day Ockfener Bockstein), where they had been clearing about 15 hectares of oak coppices on a steep slate slope, as was later done on an even larger scale in Serrig (Vogelsang and Schiessberg), a little upriver, and Avelsbach (Hammerstein and Rotlei), in a side valley between Trier and the lower Ruwer. Ripper reports that more than 70 hectares of *Lohhecken* had been cleared and planted in Riesling vines around the districts of Saarburg and Trier. By 1906, some of the other notable hillsides cleared of woods and planted to vines included Würtzberg in Serrig, Schlangengraben in Wiltingen, Karlsberg in Oberemmel, Falkenstein and de Nysberg in Niedermennig, and Schlossberg in Sommerau. (The sparkling-wine producer Adolf Wagner first planted Schloss Saarfelser Schlossberg in Serrig in 1912; it is solely owned by Vereinigte Hospitien today.)

Mosel Riesling tended to have a pale yellow-green tint and was often described as airy, zesty, and naturally *spritzig*, or slightly effervescent. Another popular term for Mosel wine during this period was *göhrig*, which seems to have connoted fermentation aromas (yeastiness), piquancy, vivacity from dissolved CO_2, and pure taste. Where today, among the better growers, average ripeness for nonbotrytis Riesling is anywhere from 80 to 95 degrees Oechsle, a measure of sugar in the grapes, back then the average ripeness in lesser vintages ranged from 65 to 85 degrees, and, for botrytised grapes for sweet wines, up to 110 degrees in a good vintage, and rarely more. Producers vinified quickly at cool temperatures—easier in an era when harvest seldom took place before late October—avoiding contact with air, to keep the crispness, the CO_2, and the pure saltiness of Riesling from slate. Unlike the dominant Rheingau practice, Mosel growers tried to pick the late-ripening Riesling grapes at full ripeness but before botrytis set in and they pressed the grapes on the same day, to retain the green color—the so-called Mosel green—along with the freshness and liveliness. In contrast to other regions, noble rot was seen as undesirable, because it affected the wine's color, aroma, and taste.

Before 1860, the yields per vine had been higher and the grapes less carefully selected at harvest. Unlike large landowners, small growers—who, on average, had 15 or more noncontiguous parcels—didn't always have Riesling, much less the knowledge, time, or means to pick their grapes late and in multiple passes. Where previously the grapes had been crushed—sometimes with a hand-cranked mill set on top of an open wooden vat in the vineyard—and left with the skins for one or more days in the press house, leading to more golden-colored wines, by the latter half of the 19th century, such skin contact was frowned upon (except when it came to Auslesen, made from selectively harvested riper grapes). In the Rheingau and other regions, the mash was typically set aside until the first bubbles appeared, to extract more aromatics and substance. (The Rheingau was known for three types of Auslesen—from overripe grapes, from botrytised grapes, and from the dried, shriveled, botrytised grapes that made Trockenbeerenauslesen.) Ripper writes that Mosel wine was made to keep its effusive bouquet, in contrast to Rhine wine. That meant less contact with oxygen, such as during pressing and racking (taking the wine off its lees into another cask). Minimal handling, along with the deep, cool, damp cellars, helped the wine to retain some of the natural CO_2 from fermentation, and if need be, a small dose of liquid CO_2 could even be injected into the cask, in an effort to enliven older, allegedly "tired" wine.

Except for the well-known Mosel estates that released their wines for auction after one or two years in *Fuder*, most of the wines were sold by cask to wholesalers and bottled earlier to keep them fresh and zappy. That was more easily done in the Mosel than the warmer Pfalz, Nahe, Rheingau, or Rheinhessen, where the grapes from the best sites were generally riper and the acidity lower. Nowadays, many German Rieslings are bottled within a few months of the harvest, the majority after five or six months, because of the wine style and demand for the newest vintage.

Further, various estates and contract bottlers, and not only in the Mosel, use a device, such as Carbofresh, to inject CO_2, but the taste isn't quite the same as with residual CO_2 from fermentation. Also to ensure freshness, more and more producers are switching to screwcaps, especially for entry-level wines, because of lower costs and worry about cork taint, but the CO_2 can stand out a bit, and some wines can have accentuated reduced notes, such as rubber and "struck flint," and in the most extreme instances, like rotten eggs.

In *Moselwein,* published in 1897, Karl Heinrich Koch asks, "What explains the popularity of Mosel wine? Could it have emerged so overwhelmingly if it were only a mere fad?" He says, "Formerly, the public made short work of judging Mosel wines, which were constantly being compared to Rhine wines. Rhine wine is sweet; Mosel wine is sour: that was an unshakable axiom." Ripper in fact quotes Koch as describing Mosel wine with an array of adjectives: pale, aromatic, spicy, floral, delicate, piquant, elegant, steely, racy, fresh, and crisp.

Koch was a wine broker and wine author, and at the time of his Mosel book he was secretary of the German Sparkling Wine Producers in Wiesbaden. But he says the racy Mosel wines were in fashion even in the wine bars of Mainz, where he lived and which had formerly served only the rich, soft wines of the Rheinhessen's hinterland. The praise of Mosel wine went so far as to prompt Nicola Racke—a prominent Mainz wine merchant, auctioneer, and former politician at the Reichstag—to complain in a letter to the editor of the Mainz weekly *Weinbau und Weinhandel* that an 1897 report on the Trier wine auctions unfairly downplayed Rhine wine. Racke pointed out that the top wines from the Rheingau still achieved much higher prices than the Mosel, despite all the hype surrounding Mosel wine.

Koch wrote other books on German wine, including on the Rheingau and Rheinhessen, and he worked for several years with a Rhenish cooper, who, he says, had an exceptionally gifted palate. When the cooper tasted a wine in the easy, brisk style, he summarized his assessment in just two words: *"er zappelt"*—"it's zappy." In other words, the wine—in this case, Mosel—animates you to, among other things, drink more. That was the cooper's highest praise.

"Er lockelt"—"it entices" (prompts you to take the next sip)—was another common description of Mosel. Koch describes the wine's aroma as unfolding, a part of the character of the Riesling from slate, and he says Mosel expresses this enticement better than any other wine. Koch wasn't a snob, either, because his praise included simple Mosel wines, such as those from the less well-known villages of the Lower Mosel. Ripper also says that Mosel distinguishes itself with its delicate, flowery bouquet and its uniquely tasty acidity. (Back then health benefits were also attributed to Mosel, particularly for treating stone, kidney, and urine ailments. "Caseler" wines were especially sought after.) Today, many producers and drinkers have an aversion to high acidity. And yet (ripe) acidity is associated with some of the finest flavors, and some of the most discriminating wine drinkers look for it for that reason.

At the all-important Mosel wine auctions in Trier, such as in 1895, 1896, and 1897, many of the highest-priced wines came from the Saar, whose "wines are generally credited with displaying the most noble of Riesling bouquets, even more than do those of the Mosel Valley," according to Koch. "They are also leaner, more ethereal, and indeed even lighter in color, but otherwise generally of genuine Mosel character." Ripper adds that Saar wines have a more pronounced fragrance and piquant flavor of the "much-loved Riesling character" than Mosel wines do, hence the higher prices. The Saar spoke to the new taste for lucid, bracing, and refreshing wines. The November 1, 1896, issue of *Der Winzer* offers the following summary of the Saar's best vineyards: "Scharzhof with its very fine sites [Scharzhofberg and Scharzberg]; Wiltingen; Oberemmel with the outstanding Agritiusberg, Raul, and Rosenberg; Ober- and Niedermennig with Euchariusberg; in the area of Saarburg, Ockfen with the excellent sites of Geisberg and Bockstein; on the left bank, Wawern with the superb Herrenberg; Canzem; and Ayl with Neuberg." Ruwer wines from the village of Kasel—Taubenberg (in today's Nies'chen), for instance—and the famous vineyards of Karthäuserhofberg and Maximin Grünhäuser Herrenberg (in what is now Abtsberg), all three in small side valleys, were similar in style to those of the Saar and similarly high-priced.

Compared with the Middle and Lower Mosel, the Saar and Ruwer are higher and somewhat windier and cooler, despite being farther south. In addition to vineyards, they feature rolling countryside with forests, pastures, and other crops. The Saar and Ruwer also had important landowners with large, contiguous, and more efficient vineyards, as opposed to the more parceled holdings of the Middle Mosel. In 1898, Friedrich Wilhelm Koch (no relation to Karl Heinrich Koch), who was director of viticulture for the Rhine Province, wrote in *Die Weine im Gebiete der Mosel und Saar* (The Wines in the Region of the Mosel and Saar) that most of the best sites on the Saar, not all of which are steep, are in side valleys. He cited, in this order, Bockstein, Geisberg, Scharzhofberg, Scharzberg (now a part of the enlarged Scharzhofberg), Raul, Oberemmel, Euchariusberg, Wawerner Herrenberg, Ayler Kupp, and a large part of the district of Wiltingen. F.W. Koch and H. Stephanus' text accompanied their detailed map of the Mosel and Saar, which differed markedly in form and aims from Clotten's 1868 Saar and Mosel tax map and from Eduard Markworth's 1897 Lower Mosel tax map of the administrative district of Koblenz. (F.W. Koch was an expert on the Mosel and Saar. Ripper highlights the "exquisite" books from both Kochs, neither of whom thought a classification of Mosel vineyards was feasible.) Saar Rieslings, often termed "steely" or "racy," like those of the Ruwer, tend to be lighter, crisper, and higher in acidity with more apple and citrus flavors, because of the warm days and even cooler nights that help preserve flavors and acidity.

On the Mosel during this era, the only designation used to indicate a level of ripeness was Auslese. Wines so designated tended to have more body and less acidity than we nowadays associate with Mosel Riesling Auslese. A common term for such *naturreine,* or "naturally pure," wines was *Kreszenz,* which indicated estate-grown grapes and applied to the unadulterated Mosel and Saar wines, and not just Auslesen, that Ripper tasted at the congress, including some of his favorites, like the 1895 Scharzhofberger from Egon Müller, 1895 Geisberger from Adolf Rheinart, and 1897 Maximiner Grünhäuser Herrenberger from Freiherr von Stumm-Halberg. Back then, Mosel wines (often listed under the village name rather than the hillside or site) were almost never labeled Spätlese, or "late harvest," much less Kabinett (which was more frequently spelled "Cabinet"), a term of approbation long used in designating the Rheingau's finest reserve wines, including Auslesen, such as the famous and expensive

Schloss Johannisberger and Steinberger. Another common practice during this time was adding sugar water, called Gallizing, to the unfermented grape juice to improve underripe, high-acid Riesling. For "natural wines" (*Naturweine*), this practice or the direct addition of plain sugar before or during fermentation, known as chaptalization, was considered unacceptable. The same applied to fining agents and de-acidification. Although purists, especially on the Saar, condemned sugared wines, this "improvement" helped small growers make palatable wines in poor vintages and expanded the market for Mosel wine.

The old books and wine lists suggest that Mosel wine is best consumed in the first ten years, whereas the residually sweet Mosel Rieslings deemed classic today by many producers and connoisseurs are often at their best only after ten or more years in bottle. (Not that today's dry Mosels can't age that long!) There's little doubt that a few of the highest-priced Mosels, such as the renowned 1893 Maximin Grünhäuser Herrenberger *Fuder No. 53*, the most expensive Mosel wine of the time, were affected by noble rot to the point where, when the wine ceased fermenting, it was left with considerable residual sugar. But "classic" in those days meant dry.

In the 1890s, the green-tinted, light-bodied, and, for the most part, dry-tasting Mosel wines were in fashion, and not only in Germany but also around the world. The taste was for spritzy wines that go down well, and no other region could produce this style of wine better than the Mosel. Mosel wine by its very nature tends to be fragrant, fresh, bright, light, and invigorating, provided it comes from a good slate vineyard, isn't picked too ripe, and is fermented fairly dry without additives and extended skin contact. The best sites tend to be on south-facing slopes (though that's changing some with global warming). The key is Riesling and the mystery of Mosel slate. ◆

Added Notes on Some Important Saar and Ruwer Vineyards

by Lars Carlberg

An 1896 article, "Mosel- und Saarweine," in the Trier weekly *Der Winzer* highlighted both the Saar and Ruwer for the recent quality of their wines. Places on the Ruwer "with very favorable sites" included Karthäuserhof, Grünhaus, Kasel, and Waldrach. Saar wines, which had been sold as "Mosel wines," were brought to market under their own name due to their distinctive excellence, such as those from Scharzhof and Ockfen (see page 64). These notes provide more detail about some of these places.

Ayler Kupp Neuberg is a site within Ayler Kupp and was at one time a new part of the hill planted to vines, hence the name "new hill." On Clotten's 1868 tax map, Neuberg, colored light red, designates primarily the main south-facing slope in the *Gewann* Im untersten Berg, which comprises (from top to bottom) "Stirn" and "Unterstenberg." Throughout the 19th century, the area planted to vines in the original Ayler Kupp, as depicted on Clotten's map, was only about 17 ha. The tapered half of the slope, facing southwest, including the tail end *Gewann* Wald ("forest"), was cleared and planted at different stages in the first part of the 20th century. The hillside now has about 34 ha of vineyards. In 1898, the best-known producer was Dr. Görtz in Trier. He was the heir to Frau Oberförster Linz (née Görtz) in Ayl and continued the tradition of auctioning his family's wines by the *Fuder* as "Ayler Herrenberger," which, back then, came from separate parcels of ca. 9 ha. Since 1927, Bischöfliches Konvikt possesses these choice vineyards. The large middle parcel, called "Grosser Herrenberg," abuts "im untersten

Berg," where Konvikt also has vines, and corresponds to the then place name "im neuen Berg" ("in the new hill") on an old cadastral map of Ayl. (A long flight of stairs now marks the border between these two subsites.) The name "Herrenberg" would later designate this core area, whereas the section of the slope towards Wawern, including a 1.3-ha new planting, would be marked as "Neuberg" on Clotten's 1906 map. Today's 4.6-ha *Einzellage* Ayler Herrenberger, solely owned by Konvikt, is on the upper, steeper slope in the *Gewann* Im Neuenberg but farther west (not to be confused with "im neuen Berg"). In 1884, Bischöfliches Priesterseminar purchased from A.D. Pescatore of Luxembourg the coveted ca. 3-ha slice on the rounded hill, or *Kuppe*, closer to the river, and auctioned its wines either as "Ayler" or "Ayler Kupp." (In 1966, the two Trier seminaries merged with the Trier Cathedral to form the Bischöfliche Weingüter Trier.) Since 1971, the 49.2-ha *Einzellage* Ayler Kupp has been among numerous vastly expanded "single sites" and includes the hillsides Scheidterberg, Rauberg, Schonfels, and Sonnenberg. According to F.W. Koch's *Weine*, the villages of Ayl, Wawern, and Kanzem had wines that fetched significantly higher prices at auction by the latter half of the 19th century.

Bockstein Since 1983, Ockfener Bockstein refers to the entire hillside. Before then, the sites and later *Einzellagen* included Ockfener Kupp, Herrenberg, Heppenstein, Bockstein, Zickelgarten, and Neuwies. The mostly steep upper slope, parts of which were abandoned and covered with scrub several years ago, was still largely coppiced woodland in 1890. These include, from west to east: the *Gewanne* Herrenberg (planted by A. Rheinart around 1890 and named Ober-Herrenberg until 1971), Heppenstein, Bockstein (i.e., the large parcel above the upper mid-slope path that extends from Domäne Ockfen, built in 1902, to the summit cross on the rugged granite outcrop), and Oberst Bockstein, farther east. Lower down the slope and closer to the river, the less known Kupp vineyard is now shrubs and trees. On Clotten's 1868 tax map, the top sites in the greater Bockstein, picked out in dark red, are the westernmost Herrenberg (i.e., *Gewann* Im Herrenberg, below Ober-Herrenberg) and the easternmost Bockstein and Neuwies. Wines from each were once sold separately as Herrenberger, Bocksteiner, and Neuwieser. The eastern sector of Bockstein includes, among other *Gewanne*, Bockstein hinter der langen Rausch, Im Bockstein, and Bockstein, the latter of which corresponding to what became known as Ockfener Bockstein-Zickelgarten and later shortened to Ockfener Zickelgarten in the mid-20th century. The revised 1890 edition of Clotten's map also places a dark-red fleck, indicating a top site, around the *Gewann* Im Jung in the central part of Bockstein. (Wines labeled "Bocksteiner" also came from this part of the slope above the village, such as those from Forstmeister Geltz.) The 1906 edition shows the vineyard expansion higher up the hill. Bockstein now has a total of 52.9 ha. Nearly all of the Saar's best sites are on slopes with southern exposures in side valleys, and all the ones marked dark red are on the right bank, from Geisberg in the south to Euchariusberg in the north. The predominantly gray slate on many of these south-facing slopes contains quartz and quartzite-bearing sandstone.

Euchariusberg The historic Euchariusberg hillside, marked dark red on Clotten's map, is also known as Großschock (or Gross Schock). More specifically, Großschock is a place name, or *Gewann*, that designates the ca. 5-ha south-facing slope and was the only area on that high hill and neighboring hills to be planted to vines already in the early 1800s. The hillside's deep gray clayey-slate soil is mixed with quartz and quartzite-bearing sandstone. A little farther south, in Obermennig, is Kapellenberg (a part of the greatly expanded 36-ha *Einzellage* Krettnacher Euchariusberg, most of which faces west or west to southwest, as does the adjoining 4-ha *Einzellage* Niedermenniger Euchariusberg on the principal hill). Between 1803 and 1813, Jean Joseph Tranchot and his team of engineer-geographers began to topographically map the Left Bank of the Rhine for military purposes, as instructed by Napoleon. A portion of the *Gewann* Euchariusberg, facing southwest and mostly owned by von Kesselstatt, and nearly all of the *Gewann* Großschock were listed as "Kruschock" on Tranchot's 1812 map of the area. The engineer-geographers Kolb and Bagetti mapped this area of the Saar, whereas the engineer-geographer Filhon rendered the 1812 map of Saarburg and environs (see note on Saarburg below). Karl Freiherr von Müffling completed the series of maps under Prussian rule from 1816 to 1820 and produced supplementary sheets of the Rhineland from 1826 to 1828.

Geisberg Along with having replanted large parts of the south-facing slopes in Wawern (Goldberg), Oberemmel (the former Junkerberg), and other villages of the Saar, Van Volxem is now recultivating ca. 14 ha in the once famous Geisberg, a steep slope to the east of Bockstein—where Van Volxem has also taken over many vineyards in recent years—and rich in quartzite-laden sandstone. Geisberg first appears on Clotten's 1890 map; the prime south-facing slope had no more than 10 ha of vineyards then, with the lower western half (*Gewann* Dollbüsch), planted around 1850 (and again in 2020), colored dark red. Geisberg was greatly expanded to over 50 ha, as depicted on Clotten's 1906 map. In the 1890s, the top producers of Geisberg included C. Gebert, A. Rheinart, Kerckhoff, Amlinger-Keller, and Geltz. All of them had vineyards in the famous Bockstein and, except for Gebert, had cellars in Saarburg. In 1902, Friedrich-Wilhelm-Gymnasium, Geltz, and J. Wagner bought at auction newly cleared land in Geisberg. Friedrich-Wilhelm-Gymnasium built a press house (now a ruin) in Geisberg in 1910, as it had done previously in de Nysberg, now known as Falkensteiner Hofberg, in 1901. The excellent wines from Rheinart's new planting in Ober-Herrenberg (*Gewann* Herrenberg) helped inspire the Prussian government to establish Domäne Ockfen and to plant vines, starting in 1896, on the upper slope in Heppenstein and Bockstein, which by 1902 totaled 15 ha, plus another 39 ha in Schiessberg-Serrig. During this time, Graf von Kesselstatt and the brewery owner Gustav Vanvolxem, who also had vines in Kasel, planted various new Saar vineyards. Just south of Ockfen is the south-facing slope of Fröhn (*Gewann* In der Fröhn), or Fröhnert, whose potential is not to be overlooked and is now a part of the *Einzellagen* Saarburger Klosterberg and Irscher Sonnenberg. In the 1890s, Frau Wwe. N. Orth auctioned her Saarburger, Bocksteiner, and Fröhner wines in Trier.

Maximin Grünhaus In 1882, Carl Ferdinand Stumm, a Prussian coal and steel industrialist from the Saarland, purchased Maximin Grünhaus for the price of 600,000 marks. After Stumm was ennobled in 1888, the estate became known as Freiherrlich von Stumm-Halberg'sche Rittergutsverwaltung Grünhaus. (His eldest daughter, Ida, later received the estate as a part of her dowry, when she married the Prussian Lieutenant General Conrad von Schubert.) It consisted of 11 ha of vineyards, among other property; in the 1890s, the average net yield was about 38 *Fuder*. Freiherr von Stumm-Halberg auctioned 26 *Fuder* of his 1893 Maximiner Grünhäuser Herrenberger, two of which set record prices. The primary vineyard at Grünhaus (in the *Gewann* Grünhäuserberg) was Herrenberg, whose lower to mid-slope (starting at the conical prominence) is colored dark red on Clotten's tax map. The name "Maximiner-Grünhäuser-Herrenberg" is inscribed on the stone portal from 1873 that stands at the foot of what in the mid-20th century began to be referred to as Maximin Grünhäuser Herrenberg-Abtsberg and then simply as Abtsberg (14 ha), whereas the name "Herrenberg" began getting applied to the tapered slope west, favoring a deeper reddish soil, compared with the bluish-gray slate of the original Maximin Grünhäuser Herrenberg. The *Gewann* that corresponds to today's Herrenberg is Im Viertelsberg, also spelled Im Viertelberg. (The *Viertel*, or "quarter-share," of crop was what tenants owed to St. Maximin's after laity were granted permission in 1579 to clear and plant that part of the slope.) In Koch's time, the tail end of the slope was not yet planted, unlike the east-facing Bruderberg vineyard. Today, after enlargements that include a 10-ha 1976 extension onto the plateau of Grüneberg (assigned to the *Einzellage* Herrenberg), the estate has an impressive 34 ha of vines. Bischöfliches Konvikt, Walther Mittelstrass (formerly Joh. Rheinart), and Frau Wwe. Dominik Nau all in Koch's time once auctioned casks of Grünhäuser. In the 1880s, Joh. Rheinart's Grünhäuser were designated as coming from Viertelberg. Bischöfliches Konvikt had most of its holdings in the Ruwer Valley—namely, 4 ha of vineyards at Hofgut Duisburg (Duisburger Hof) in Eitelsbach and 7 parcels with about 40,000 vines on the Grünhaus hillside in Mertesdorf, as well as another 40,000 vines in Kasel.

Raul Like Agritiusberg and Rosenberg, Raul is a largely forgotten but once highly rated site in Oberemmel. Adjacent to Raul, on the same slope, are the old sites (from west to east): Lautersberg, Hütte, Elzerberg, and Junkerberg (a part of today's *Einzellage* Oberemmeler Altenberg). On Clotten's 1890 map, the area between Raul and Elzerberg, which includes the prized Lautersberg and Hütte, is shown in dark red without gaps. The site name "Hütte" is first listed on the 1906 edition. The post-1971 5.8-ha *Einzellage* Oberemmeler Hütte, solely owned by von Hövel, includes both Lautersberg and Elzerberg, and the 2.2-ha *Einzellage* Oberemmeler Raul, where von Kesselstatt once owned vines, comprises the *Gewanne* Raul and Im Raul on the far western edge of the south-facing slope.

Saarburg By 1890, the main vineyard areas of Saarburg comprised Schlossberg, an east-to-southeast-facing slope adjacent to the castle ruin, and today's Saarburger Rausch, which, since 2011, encompasses the former *Einzellagen* Saarburger Antoniusbrunnen and Bergschlösschen, once called Mühlberg. As a result, Rausch expanded from 8.7 to 22.7 ha. This large hillside, known as Saarburgerberg, rises directly behind the town and was completely covered by vines in 1812, unlike many other south-facing slopes on the Saar. In contrast to Ockfen, no Saarburg sites were highly rated during Koch's time, despite the significance of the town to the wine trade and the presence of prominent producers, such as Wwe. N. Orth, Jos. Heinr. Wagner, and Forstmeister Geltz, the last two in Beurig (and notwithstanding the high quality nowadays associated with this slope, especially as rendered at Forstmeister Geltz Zilliken and Dr. Wagner). Per F.W. Koch's seminal 1898 *Weine*, the present-day Rausch occupied classes 5 to 7 out of 8 for tax purposes, a status unchanged in the posthumous 1914 update of Koch's text. The two sites, or *Lagen*, he lists first, parts of which are in the area colored light red on Clotten's tax map, are Auf der Laienkaul (Layenkaul) and In der Schul; just to the east of here and lower down his list are the adjoining well-sited place names Rauschboden and higher up the hill Auf der Rausch—a sector on the prominent conical part of the slope, known as "Franzens Knüppchen," that according to geologists features a high proportion of so-called green stone, or diabase, mixed with gray slate. (A Prussian geological map, from

1877, shows several diabase intrusions in the upper section of today's Saarburger Rausch but also in other slate slopes of the lower Saar, in particular the western part of Krettnacher Altenberg. See note 65.) F.W. Koch wrote at the beginning of *Weine*, which covers the Saar region first, that the extremely hard *"Beinigers"* is a volcanic rock, but he is surely referring to *Diabas* instead of *Beinerling*, a quartzite-bearing sandstone, although the latter is also hard and unique to certain sites on the Saar. Down by the river, Laurentiusberg, which already had vines in 1812 and lies fallow on Clotten's 1868 and 1890 editions, reappears as a new planting on the 1906 edition.

Scharzhofberg The "new" Scharzberg vineyard—primarily situated on the slope to the east of the Scharzhof manor in the direction of Oberemmel—is now part of the enlarged 28.1-ha Scharzhofberg (which, technically, is *einzellagenfrei*, or not designated as an *Einzellage*). The lower hump of the hill marks the old Scharzhofberg's eastern border with the new Scharzberg. Egon Müller and von Hövel, formerly Frau Wwe. Jos. Grach, have parcels in this former site. "Scharzberg"—not to be confused with the 729-ha *Grosslage* Scharzberg, which took its name and encompasses the whole Saar region—is sometimes used to refer to the entire hill, as listed in dark red on Clotten's map. On Tranchot's 1812 map, the eastern and upper sections of "Chartzberg" in what would later become the Scharzberg vineyard, including the *Gewann* Höchste Pergentsknopp, where Van Volxem and von Kesselstatt have parcels at the crest of the hill, were yet to be planted with vines. The VDP has declared the Pergentsknopp subsite—which includes the southwest-facing part of "Knipp" in the *Gewann* In Pergentsknoepp (above the Vols sector of Wiltinger Braunfels) and is mostly owned by Egon Müller—as a "Grosse Lage." (The VDP also classified as Grosse Lage a part of Braunfels, under the name "Volz.") In Koch's era, two of the most famous producers of Scharzhofberger (pre-1971 18 ha) and Scharzberger were Geschwister Apollinar Koch, who had vine plantings known as "Altscharzer Riesling," and Egon Müller at Scharzhof. An old path that only ran through a part of the upper slope divided these two sites. The vineyards below the path were Scharzhofberg and those above it (i.e., Pergentsknopp) Scharzberg. The

Trier Cathedral, or the *Hohe Domkirche,* owns the old part of Scharzhof, *Alter Scharzhof,* since 1851 and regularly auctioned its wines as either "Dom-Scharzhofberger" or "Scharzhofberger." The "new" Scharzhof, where Egon Müller resides, was erected in the 1880s and remodeled after a fire destroyed the roof of the south wing and the upper floor of the tower in 1917. Today, the largest holding, 8.5 ha in different parts of the south-facing slope, belongs to Egon Müller, including this renowned site's last remaining block of ungrafted old vines (ca. 2.2 ha) still trained on single wooden stakes in "Breiten Weinberg" in the *Gewann* aptly named Im Besten Scharzberg ("in the best Scharzberg"); all the other parcels in Scharzhofberg have wire trellises. The second-largest vineyard holding, with 6.6 ha, in Scharzhofberg belongs to von Kesselstatt, which added to its already impressive portfolio on this hill the vineyards from Apollinar Koch. The Hohe Domkirche, a part of Bischöfliche Weingüter Trier, possesses various well-sited parcels, two of which are behind the manor and border Egon Müller's ungrafted old vines; the church's total holdings of 6.3 ha is the third largest in Scharzhofberg. This is followed by von Hövel with 2.85 ha, most of which is in the former Scharzberg site, farther east, except for a tiny plot in the original Scharzhofberg. Van Volxem and Vereinigte Hospitien have 2 ha each. The hillside has a deep soil of weathered gray clayey slate with more so-called graywacke in the less steep eastern part of the slope. The east end is a part of the expanded *Einzellage* Oberemmeler Rosenberg, which, like Ayler Kupp, includes a number of hillsides since 1971. The original Rosenberg is listed as "Rosenkamm" on Clotten's map.

A Short Glossary of the
Amazingly Complicated German
Vineyard Designations

❖

We worry, for example: "Will the reader understand that 'Piesporter Falkenberg' is an official 'single site,' or *Einzellage*, stretching over much of the upper half of the steep slope in Piesport, whereas the old site name 'Falkenberg,' as listed on Clotten's tax map, refers to a much smaller surface area, a site (*Lage*) adjacent to today's *Einzellage* Piesporter Schubertslay and not even located in today's enlarged Falkenberg?" Moreover, the cadastral place name, or *Gewannname*, "Im Falkenberg" corresponds more or less—but not precisely—to the old site. Often a former site, such as Himmelreich in Graach, lies within the much-expanded official *Einzellage* of the same name. But in the case of Goldtröpfchen, the old site matches the *Gewann* Auf Dambesmauer, which, like Im Weer, is actually in the *Einzellage* Piesporter Domherr (see note 93). In contrast, Taubengarten (*Gewann* Aufm Taubengarten) is one of the best sites in today's Goldtröpfchen but is not even listed on the 1906 edition of Clotten's map. This glossary is meant to make the complications at least a little bit clearer.

Alleinbesitz A vineyard with a sole owner, the same as French *monopole*— Maximin Grünhäuser Abtsberg or Enkircher Batterieberg, for instance.

Einzellage An official "single-vineyard" site. An *Einzellage* nearly always includes the *Ortsname*, or village name, with the suffix *-er*, plus the site name—e.g., Dhroner Hofberg, meaning the site of Hofberg in the village of Dhron. To add confusion, the VDP prefers that its "Grosse Lagen" ("great sites")—in copyrighted all-caps form as VDP.GROSSE LAGE®—appear without their attendant village name, so as to resemble *grand cru* vineyards in Burgundy's Côte d'Or. Thus a producer uses the legally required label with the village plus site, and then you turn the bottle around and see the showier presentation label on the other side with the site but not the village! In the Mosel, the 1971 Wine Law reduced the number of sites, some of which first appeared (with the requisite village name attached) in the 20th century, from nearly 10,000 to, currently, 524 official single vineyards, or *Einzellagen*. (The same occurred in other German wine regions.) In most cases, an *Einzellage* comprises many formerly designated *Lagen*—often less well known, even ones on an entirely different slope. And many of these newly expanded *Einzellagen* took the noblest names that were simply transferred from a once famous site on a steep slope (e.g., Piesporter Treppchen and Erdener Bußlay) to flat land. The official "Treppchen" vineyard in Piesport covers nearly the entire alluvial plain on the opposite bank of the Mosel from the old town. With few exceptions, an *Einzellage* must be larger than 5 hectares. Some that were designated in 1971 have officially ceased to exist because they fell out of use for an extended period (e.g., Ockfener Zickelgarten; see note 55) or because the producers in a community elected to amalgamate sites (e.g., Saarburger Antoniusbrunnen and Bergschlösschen were subsumed under Saarburger Rausch, which had become better known by the early 21st century). A new *Einzellage* must be federally registered in a rigorous, time-consuming process, usually initiated by an individual proprietor.

Gewächs "Growth," similar to French *cru* (see note 16). In Germany, this term is nowadays seldom used on its own, but it does appear as part of "Grosses Gewächs," or GG, especially within the VDP, to designate a legally dry wine—which can be chaptalized, of all things—from an ostensibly top site, or "Grosse Lage," (effectively, a *"grand cru"*). *Spitzengewächs* translates as "top growth."

Gewann (Gewannname) A place name, equivalent to a French *lieu-dit*, for a small section on the cadastral map. Very often, the current official place name and the old unofficial one for a specific site (*Lage*) are nearly identical and refer more or less to the identical area. (But not all former site names are place names, and many former sites comprised various place names.) The difference in name frequently comes down to a preposition—e.g., the site within the *Einzellage* Ürziger Würzgarten commonly referred to and written as "Kranklay" (also spelled "Kranklai") has the official cadastral name "In der Kranklei." Since the 2014 vintage, a producer may register an official cadastral place name for use on wine labels, where it must be joined with the name of the commune. Including the official *Einzellage* is optional for the time being. So, for example, a wine could be labeled "Ürziger Würzgarten In der Kranklei" or simply "Ürziger In der Kranklei."

Grosslage A collective site, of which there are 19 in the Mosel, created by the 1971 Wine Law employing old site names (*Lagenamen*) and composed of multiple *Einzellagen*. While the notion of a collective site existed previously, the confusion engendered by *Grosslagen* was part of their design: a name implying high quality acts as an umbrella covering mixed sites. For example, "Piesporter Goldtröpfchen" is an *Einzellage* within the commune of Piesport and represents some of the Middle Mosel's most prestigious surface area for planting Riesling. "Piesporter Michelsberg" is a *Grosslage* that straddles eight communes and incorporates 35 *Einzellagen* (only 10 of which are in the commune of Piesport), some of marginal significance, some even in today's warming climate incapable of ripening Riesling. The recently introduced VDP-designation "Grosse Lage" ("great site") can only add to the confusion.

Katasterlage A cadastral site, or *Gewann*.

Kreszenz "Growth" (see note 5).

Lage A specific vineyard site, similar to *climat* in Burgundy, whether official or unofficial. Both unofficial site names and unregistered place names (*Gewannnamen*) sometimes still appear on wine labels—the authorities usually request the producer to cease and desist.

Monopollage A *monopole* site.

Ort A village or town. Until the 1909 Wine Law, labels generally didn't give a site name but just the village name (*Ortsname*), such as "Piesporter," even for the top sites. (As a case in point, Frau M. Felzen auctioned her 5 to 9 *Fuder* simply as "Piesporter," not as "Piesporter Schubertslay," which first appeared around 1920. Ditto the wines from von Kesselstatt, which came from different sites in Piesport.) Now that the VDP is copying the Burgundy model, an *Ortswein* ("village wine") implies a wine lower down in the classification pyramid, even if it comes from a top site.

Further Reading

A sampling of useful works.

Beck, Otto. *Der Weinbau an der Mosel und Saar.* Trier, Kgl. Regierung, 1869.

Deckers, Daniel. *Im Zeichen des Traubenadlers: Eine Geschichte des deutschen Weins.* Mainz, von Zabern, 2010.

—————————. *The Sign of the Grape and Eagle: A History of German Wine.* Frankfurt, Frankfurt Academic Press, 2018.

—————————. *Historische Lagenkarten.* vdp.de, 2021.

Fisch, Jean, and David Rayer. "The Vineyard Classification Before the 1850s." moselfinewines.com, Issue No. 39. Jan. 2018.

—————————. "Mosel Wine in the 19th Century." moselfinewines.com, Issue No. 49. Jan. 2020.

Gerdolle, Heinrich. *Der Weinbau in Lothringen.* In: Das Reichsland Elsass-Lothringen. Theil 1. Strassburg, 1898–1901.

Koch, Friedrich Wilhelm. *Der Weinbau an der Mosel und Saar.* Trier, Lintz, 1881.

Koch, Friedrich Wilhelm, and Heinrich Stephanus. *Die Weine im Gebiet der Mosel und Saar.* Trier, Heinr. Stephanus, 1898.

Koch, Karl Heinrich. *Die mittelrheinischen Handelsweine.* Mainz, von Zabern, 1893.

——————. *Zur Kritik der Weinsteuervorlage*. Mainz, von Zabern, 1893.

——————. *Das Weinland Rheinhessen*. Mainz, von Zabern, 1903.

——————. *Rheingauer Weinfahrt*. Mainz, von Zabern, 1908.

——————. *Deutsche Sektindustrie*. Mainz, von Zabern, 1923.

Krieger, Joachim. "The Mosel: Taking the Long View." Translated by Dan Melia. larscarlberg.com, Oct. 2013.

Lauer, Florian. *Die Geschichte des Ayler Weines*. lauer-ayl.de, Ausgabe 2017.

Loeb, Otto W., and Terence Prittie. *Moselle*. London, Faber, 1972.

Ripper, Maximilian. *Moselweinbau und Moselwein*. Klosterneuberg, Verlag der k.k. chemisch-physiologischen Versuchstation, 1898.

Rudd, Hugh R. *Hocks and Moselles*. London, Constable and Company Ltd., 1935.

Schoonmaker, Frank. *The Wines of Germany*. New York, Hastings House, 1956.

von Zobeltitz, Hanns. *Der Wein*. Bielefeld und Leipzig, Velhagen & Klasing, 1901.

Biographies

by Per Linder

✦━━✦━━✦

Karl Heinrich Koch was born in 1841 in Herford, in the Prussian province of Westphalia, the son of a local merchant. In the 1860s, Koch came to Mainz, where he spent the rest of his life. He quickly found his way into the wine trade. In the Mainz *Adressbuch* of 1870, he is already listed as a wine broker.

In 1874, Koch married Sophia Amalia Ohaus, a daughter of the owner of a floating bath in the Rhine River. After that, Koch ran a wine merchant business under the name Firma Koch-Ohaus. The marriage brought two daughters and a son.

Karl Heinrich Jr. was a wine merchant in Eltville and the secretary of the Association of Wine-Estate Owners in the Rheingau. In this capacity, Koch Jr. participated in the founding of the Association of German Natural Wine Auctioneers in 1910, the predecessor of the Association of German Prädikat Wine Estates, or the VDP (see Chapter 1 of Daniel Deckers' *Sign of the Grape and Eagle*, Frankfurt Academic Press, Frankfurt, 2018). He was killed in the First World War and his children were raised by Koch Sr.

Following German unification in 1871, the economy benefited from public investment in infrastructure, especially railways, which helped to grow the market for wine in Germany. This created a need for a trade press that provided information on wine auction results and legislative changes. A pioneer was the Mainz wine merchant Eduard Goldschmidt (1842–1919), who was the editor-in-chief of *Deutsche Wein-Zeitung,* a weekly whose editorials expressed the opinions of wine merchants. Around 1880, Koch himself began to work for the wine press, alongside his work as a wine merchant. He served as the managing editor of the *Wein-Halle* until the summer of 1883, when the *Deutsche Wein-Zeitung* acquired it.

At this time, Koch became closer to the Mainz publishing house Philipp von Zabern, which specialized in wine publications and in printing wine labels. He was appointed co-editor of von Zabern's *Allgemeine Wein-Revue*, a periodical linked to *Weinbau und Weinhandel*, the other major weekly Mainz-based wine periodical, which was the official organ of the Deutscher Weinbau-Verein (Association of German Winegrowers), headed by Heinrich Wilhelm Dahlen (1853–1904). This move was remarkable because the Weinbau-Verein, or at least the majority of its winegrowers, was in favor of increased trade barriers for imported wine, which was contrary to the view of most merchants. Furthermore, there was a fierce debate over many issues between the two newspapers—the *Deutsche Wein-Zeitung* and *Weinbau und Weinhandel*. A debate over the use of the famous "Steinberger" brand on labels became so contentious that it ended up in court, and Koch was commissioned to defend the publisher von Zabern.

His first book project was a translation of Arnaldo Strucchi's *Annuario generale per la viticoltura e la enologia*, which was published in 1892 under the title *Italienische Weine* (Italian Wines). The following year, he wrote his own book, *Die mittelrheinischen Handelsweine* (The Middle Rhine Wine Trade), which was a wine buyer's guide covering the Rheingau, Mittelrhein, Rheinhessen, the Nahe, and the Pfalz. The book, published by von Zabern, covered 562 wine villages and contained extensive technical information on vineyard areas, production volumes, grape varieties, and travel information. Like Friedrich Wilhelm Koch's (no relation) *Die Weine im Gebiete der Mosel und Saar* (The Wines in the Region of the Mosel and Saar, 1898), the book did not contain any illustrations. Karl Heinrich Koch wrote *Moselwein* (Mosel Wine) four years later. Although this little book was less detailed and technical, it was, in fact, beautifully illustrated (more on that below). Following his book on the Mosel, Koch wrote separate volumes on Rheinhessen (1903) and the Rheingau (1908). The latter was his best seller.

In 1894, Koch was appointed secretary of the Association of German Sparkling Wine Producers, a lobbying group, which promoted legislation to protect German sparkling wine through tariffs and restrictions on label content. In this context, it is important to point out that, legislatively, sparkling wine was treated as an industrial product, like beer, whereas wine was defined as a natural product. In concrete terms, that meant higher taxes and tariffs for sparkling wine than for wine.

Koch joined the association amidst a fight in the trade press between the Champagne producer Eugène Mercier (1838–1904) and Reichstag representative Alfred von Gescher (1844–1932). Mercier used a loophole in the German code of tariffs that allowed him to import grape must from Champagne to subsidiaries based in the area of the German Customs Union, then bottle and label it as "Champagne" and market it at a relatively low price in Germany. Such subsidiaries were considered a form of tax evasion by Koch and others at the association, who called them *Grenzfirmen* ("border firms").

The German Sparkling-Wine Producers and its secretary Koch vehemently criticized Mercier's business practices as misleading. They were, however, unsuccessful with their lobbying. The German government at the time led an export-oriented policy, introduced by Chancellor Leo von Caprivi, and was reluctant to impose further trade barriers. Only in 1925 did regulations come into force that followed the association's suggestions on labels, but by then the loophole had already become irrelevant due to World War I.

The association also actively opposed consumer taxes on sparkling wine but was unsuccessful on all the issues mentioned above during Koch's service, which he describes in his 1923 paper on the German sparkling-wine industry. Germany did introduce a sparkling-wine tax in 1902 (officially called *Schaumweinsteuer*, sometimes *Sektsteuer*) in order to finance the Imperial German Navy.

Throughout his career as a wine merchant, Karl Heinrich Koch wrote wine books as well as papers on taxation and the wine trade. He retired as a wine merchant in 1922, and six years later, in 1928, he died in Mainz at the age of 87.

Anton Lewy

Anton Josef Lewy (Antonín Lewý in Czech), the son of an Austrian customs officer, was born on March 29, 1845, in Wolfsthal, Lower Austria, on the border with then Hungary, now Slovakia. He died on September 28, 1897, in the border town and famous spa resort of Teplice (Teplitz in German), Bohemia, then part of Austria but today in the Czech Republic.

Lewy studied at the Academy of Fine Arts in Munich and later at the Academy of Fine Arts in Prague. He began his professional career in Prague, where he provided cartoons and other drawings for magazines.

Later, he shifted his focus from cartoons to landscape illustrations, the work for which he was known during the remainder of his life. From the mid-1870s, he completed many drawings of buildings in Leipzig and landscapes of Saxony. Nine of his drawings were included in an extensive guide of the Bohemian Forest.

In 1880, Lewy gave up freelancing and became a professor of drawing at a secondary school in Telpice, where he remained until his death. He continued to draw on the side—several of his drawings were published in a 24-volume work on the *Austro-Hungarian Monarchy in Word and Picture*, published in 1886.

Despite the inclusion of Lewy's work in *Moselwein*, we have no evidence that he and Koch actually collaborated on the project. Several of Lewy's Rheingau drawings were later used by the German author Hanns von Zobeltitz in his 1901 book *Der Wein*, which also reproduced many of the drawings from *Moselwein*.

Lewy's drawings in *Moselwein* were probably executed during the summer of 1896—the only drawing that is dated is the one of Scharzhofberg. The reader will note that many of the drawings seem to be co-signed "M. R. Co.," which stood for Meisenbach, Riffarth und Co., Europe's largest producer of printing plates (autotypes) at the time.

If the Czechs forgot Lewy too quickly, as his former colleagues at a Prague magazine lamented in an article two years after his death, Koch did not. In his 1908 bestselling book on the Rheingau, he used Lewy's drawing of the renowned Assmannshausen vineyard.

Contributors

Lars Carlberg works in the vineyards and cellar at Hofgut Falkenstein, where he studied as an apprentice winegrower in 2016 and 2017. He publishes the website *Lars Carlberg: Mosel Wine* (larscarlberg.com).

Kevin Goldberg, Ph.D., who was a postdoctoral fellow in international humanities at Brown University from 2011 to 2013, is chair of the history department at the Savannah Country Day School. He is the translator of *Wine Atlas of Germany* (University of California Press, 2014).

Per Linder, an amateur historian, was born and bred in Sweden and has lived in Luxembourg since 1994. He works for a family-owned investment company and has contributed articles on Mosel wine history to larscarlberg. com.

David Schildknecht has tasted his way through Germany annually since 1984. He covers its wines for *Vinous* (vinous.com) and is responsible for the entries on German wine in *The Oxford Companion to Wine*.

Yong Truong studied graphic design in Trier, where he and his wife run a concept store called Yong Yong. They offer select Mosel wines to go with an Asian cuisine prepared from fresh ingredients and based on his mother's recipes, a cuisine he has continued to refine.

Mosel

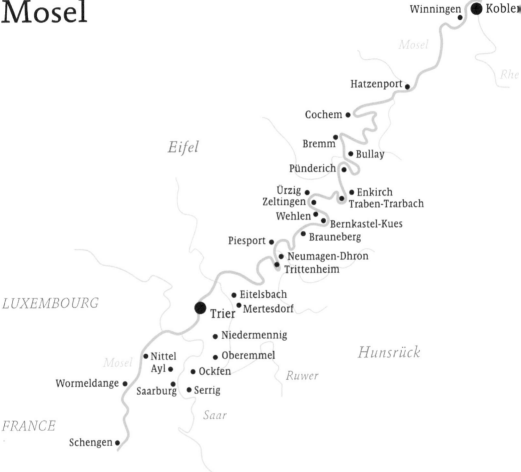

Winningen • ● Koble▸

Mosel

Rhe

Hatzenport •

Cochem •

Eifel

Bremm •
• Bullay

Pünderich •

Ürzig • • Enkirch
Zeltingen • Traben-Trarbach

Wehlen •
• Bernkastel-Kues

Piesport • • Brauneberg

• Neumagen-Dhron
Trittenheim

• Eitelsbach
Trier ● • Mertesdorf

LUXEMBOURG

• Niedermennig

• Oberemmel

Hunsrück

Mosel • Nittel
Ayl •
Wormeldange • • Ockfen
Saarburg • Serrig

Ruwer

Saar

FRANCE

Schengen •

A Note on the Type

This book was set in FF Absara, a typeface designed by Xavier Dupré, who studied graphic design in Paris and, later, calligraphy and type design at the Scriptorium de Toulouse. He first began work in 1999 as a lettering artist at a Paris design agency, and in 2001 he created his first typefaces, such as the French-style FF Parango. According to FontShop, Dupré's FF Absara (2004–2007) is also "a typeface of French proportions, but its shapes take their cues from the Dutch style: less polished, more direct." The New York Type Director's Club awarded Dupré a Certificate of Excellence for this font in 2005.

Overleaf: The 1890 edition of Franz Josef Clotten's "Viticultural Map of the Saar and Mosel." The city archive in Trier has both the 1868 and 1890 editions, but the forests are marked green only on this original copy. *Courtesy of Weingut Van Volxem.*

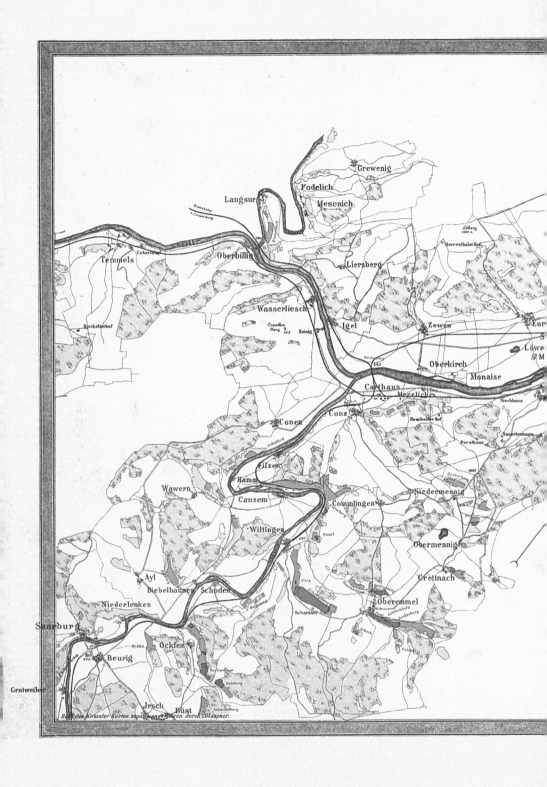

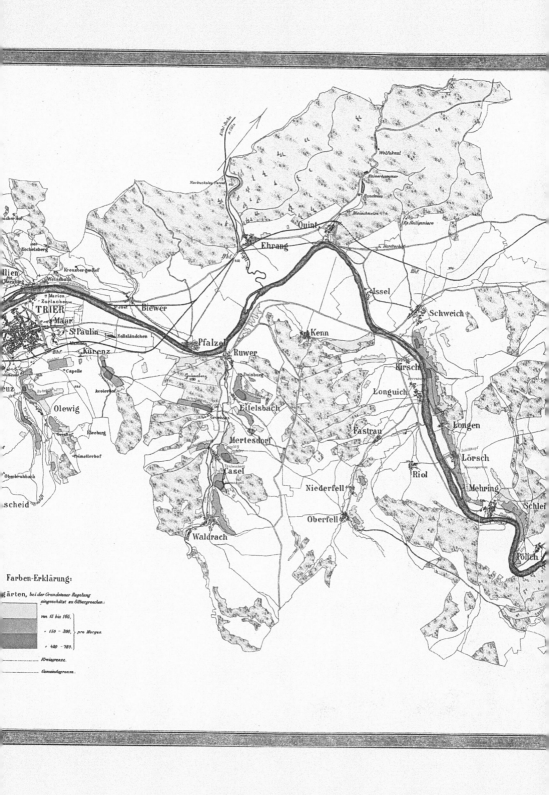

Farben-Erklärung:

gärten, *bei der Grundsteuer Regelung*
eingeschätzt zu Silbergroschen:

von 15 bis 165.

150 – 300, } pro Morgen

420 – 780.

Kreisgrenze.

Gemeindegrenze.

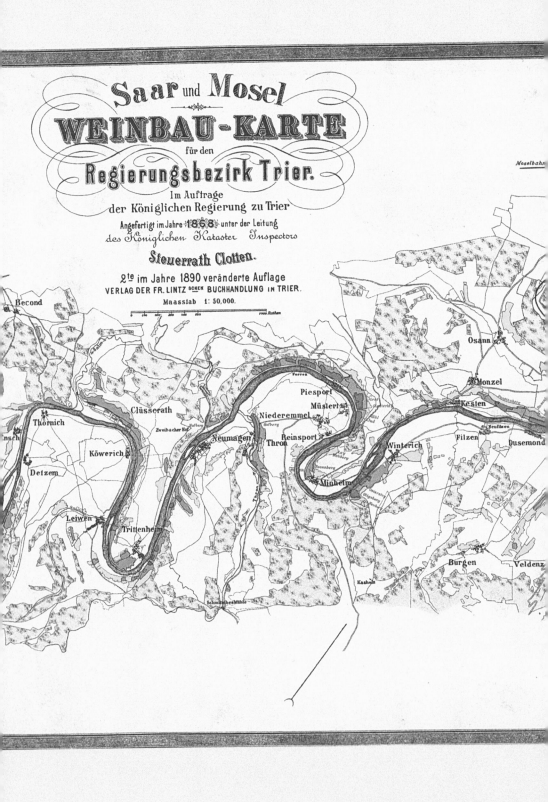

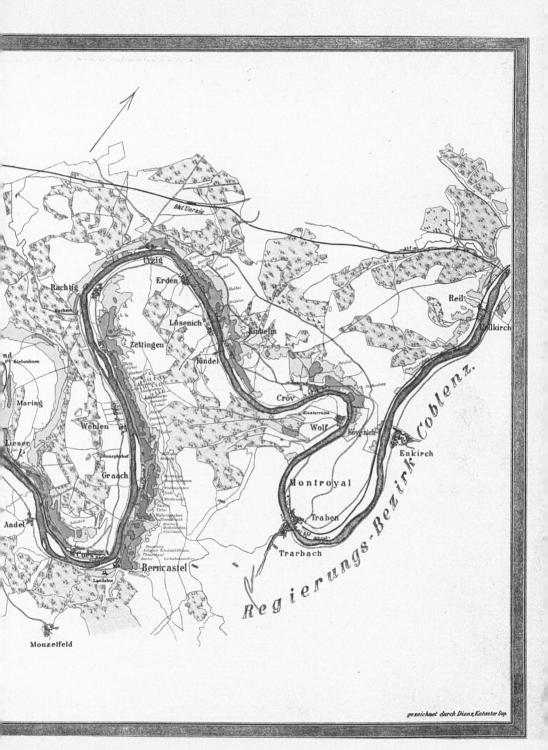

Moſelwein

—o—

Geſchrieben
von
Karl Heinrich Koch

Gezeichnet
von
Profeſſor Anton Lewy.

Dem Küfermeister Horbach, von dem ich früher so oft gehört habe „er zappelt", dediziert von Heinrich Koch

Moselwein

— ❧ —

Zu Lob und Preis des Moselweines

geschrieben

von

Karl Heinrich Koch

gezeichnet

von

Professor Anton Lewy.

Mainz

Verlag und Druck von Philipp von Zabern.

Moselwein.

Was duftet da für Duft?
Was haucht den Hauch des Maien aus
Und würzt die ganze Luft?
Zeigt her den Blumenstrauß.
        Hei, juchhei!
Im Becher funkelt Moselwein.
Bei meiner Treu, juchhei,
Nicht anders konnt' es sein.

Pfarrius.

Kellner, eine Flasche Kutscher! Der Kutscher kommt und auf der Flasche prangt das Etikett „Pies=porter." So war es noch vor dreißig Jahren in ganz Norddeutschland, wo der liebe Himmel weiß welcher Spaßvogel dem geringsten, billigsten Wein in den Gasthäusern und in den Schenken zu dem ganz allgemein gültigen Ehrentitel „Kutscher" verholfen hat. Und daß der „Kutscher" von Piesport gebürtig war, das galt so ziemlich überall als etwas Selbstverständliches. Der Moselwein war verschrieen als ein Hauptsurius, der als solcher natürlich in den Geldbeutel keine allzu große Bresche legen kann, und Piesport — nun Piesport ist ein gar so schöner und gar so besonderer Name, daß es nicht schwer fällt zu begreifen, wie er allen anderen Moselweinnamen im Bekanntwerden den Rang ablaufen mußte.

So war es vor dreißig Jahren! Und wie ist es heute? Die 1893er Piesporter Weine des Kesselstatt'schen Majorates wurden auf der zu Trier abgehaltenen Frühjahrsweinversteigerung von 1895 — es waren 38 Fuder — bezahlt mit *M.* 3270 — 4040 — 5000 — 6040 — 7070 — 9060 für das Fuder von 975 Liter, also das geringste Fuder mit *M.* 3270 (= ca. *M.* 3.35 für das Liter) und das beste Fuder mit *M.* 9060 (= ca. *M.* 9.30 für das Liter).

Noch eine andere Reminiszenz! Ich habe es selbst in den sechziger Jahren miterlebt, wie in Mainz, der Metropole des mittelrheinischen Weinhandels, kleine billige Weine von der Mosel in Schiffsladungen ankamen, nicht etwa um von hier als Moselweine in alle Welt zu gehen, sondern um verschnitten zu werden mit Rheinweinen. An der Mosel zahlte man weniger als am Rhein, so daß man mit dem Moselwein den Rheinwein billiger stellen konnte. Das sind tempi passati. Zu solchem Zwecke kommt gegenwärtig kein Tropfen Moselwein mehr nach Mainz. Aber der aufmerksame Beobachter trifft heute zuweilen auf Spuren, daß man in anderen deutschen Weinbaugebieten auf die Suche geht nach moselähnlichen Kreszenzen — so groß ist der Druck der Konkurrenz der jetzt in ihrer charakteristischen Eigenart beim Publikum beliebten Moselweine.

Die Moselweine sind Mode geworden, so sehr Mode geworden, daß sie mitten im rheinischen Weinlande beim Konsum in direkten Wettbewerb treten mit dem daselbst heimischen Produkt. Wer hätte früher wohl eine solche Neuerung für möglich gehalten, daß in Weinwirthschaften von Mainz, jener Stadt, in welcher sonst die vollen, weichen Weine des weinbautreibenden rheinhessischen Hinterlandes ausschließlich im Ausschank waren, gegenwärtig auch der rassige Moselwein in offenen Gläsern verzapft wird!

Woher kommt diese Mode? Könnte sie mit einer solchen sieghaften Allgewalt auftreten, wenn sie etwa nur einer Laune des Publikums ihr Dasein verdankte?

Ehedem war man mit dem Urtheil über die Moselweine, die immer gern in Vergleich gezogen wurden mit den Rheinweinen, schnell fertig. Der Rheinwein ist süß und der Moselwein ist sauer — das war ein Axiom, an dem nicht zu rütteln war. Diese in ihrer Einfachheit fast großartige Grundregel ist oft genug die Basis des Schiedspruches gewesen, wenn es sich darum handelte, Moselweine unter Rheinweinen herauszusuchen.

Aber man ist so allgemach dahinter gekommen, daß der Moselwein sich durch andere Eigenthümlichkeiten mehr auszeichnet als durch Säure. Man hat ihn verstehen lernen. Was hat er doch alles an sich und was nicht! Denn auch die negativen Eigenschaften spielen eine große Rolle bei der Beurtheilung des Weines; es kommt nicht blos auf die positiven an. Für die einen wie die andern verfügt der Fachmann über ein ganzes Arsenal von Bezeichnungen, die allerdings zum Theil dem Nichteingeweihten räthselhaft genug klingen. Nun läßt sich aber gerade beim Moselwein eine ganze Reihe solcher positiven und negativen Eigenschaften aufzählen, für welche ein allgemeines Verständniß vorausgesetzt werden darf, und ich kann nicht der Verlockung widerstehen, sie gegeneinander zu stellen, um auf diese Weise eine allgemeine Charakteristik des Moselweines zu geben. Man fängt vielleicht am besten mit den negativen an.

Der Moselwein ist nicht schwer, dick und voll;
er ist nicht mastig, saftig, fett und schmalzig;
er ist nicht plump und stuftig;
er ist nicht weich und läppisch;
er ist nicht stumpf und kalt;
er ist nicht matt und todt;
er ist nicht brandig;
er ist nicht hochfarbig;
er ist endlich nicht zart und lieblich und auch nicht süß, obgleich ihm gerade diese Eigenschaften gern angedichtet werden.

1*

Aber der Moselwein ist leicht und flüchtig;

er ist feingährig, duftig, blumig, würzig und piquant;

er ist elegant und süffig;

er ist fest und stahlig;

er ist rassig und charaktervoll;

er ist voller Leben, frisch, spritzig und prickelnd;

er ist lichtfarbig, grüngoldig schimmernd.

Ich habe lange Jahre mit einem rheinischen Küfermeister ✗ zusammen gearbeitet, der mit einer feinen Nase und mit einer richtigen Weinzunge begnadet war. Wenn der einen frischen, lebhaften Wein verkostete, der sonst ohne Tadel war, so faßte er sein Urtheil in die zwei Worte zusammen „er zappelt." Das war das höchste Lob, das er zu spenden pflegte. Das= selbe läßt sich ganz allgemein vom Moselwein sagen: „Er zappelt." Und dabei entfaltet er die ganze Pracht seines Aromas und seines Bouquets. Wer kann aber Aroma und Bouquet beschreiben! Das zu unternehmen, wäre ungefähr dasselbe als den Versuch zu machen, einem Blinden einen Begriff von der Farbe Blau beizubringen. Und doch lassen sich beim Moselwein einige Worte über diese flüchtigen Tugenden des Stoffes sprechen. Es ist der Charakter der Traube, der im Aroma und Bouquet des Moselweines mehr zum Ausdruck kommt als bei irgend einem anderen Wein, und eben darin liegt der eigenartige Reiz dieses Rebensaftes nicht blos für den Fachmann sondern für alle Welt. Die Mosel baut harte Traubensorten an, darunter in hervorragender Weise den Riesling, diese wunderbare deutsche Bouquettraube, wie edler auf dem ganzen Erdenrund keine andere zu finden. Das also ist bei der großen Masse des Produkts das eigentliche Kenn= zeichen des Moselweines, das Unterscheidungsmerkmal gegen andere Weine, daß ihm die auf Schieferboden gebauten harten Traubensorten das Gepräge geben, welches fest und eigen= thümlich hervortritt, weil keinerlei Zufügung von weniger charaktervollem Rebensaft aus weichen Traubensorten ab= schwächend hat wirken können.

Es ist bekannt, daß am Rhein — besonders im Rheingau, vereinzelt aber auch an anderen Stellen — Weine aus
vollständig reinem Rieslingsatz produzirt werden, und daß
vorzugsweise diesen die Rheinweine ihren alten, wohlverdienten
Ruf verdanken. Man weiß aber auch, daß der Rheingau das
klassische Gebiet der Produktion von Edelweinen aus sogenannten
edelfaulen Rieslingtrauben ist, und so unvergleichlich die in
guten Jahren daselbst erzielten Hochgewächse auch sein mögen,
so ist es doch sicher, daß die Weingewinnung aus edelfaulen
Trauben auf Kosten des besonderen Traubencharakters erfolgt.
Es werden andere höchst werthvolle Eigenschaften erzielt, aber
die eigentliche Rieslingart erleidet Einbuße.

Dagegen ist es eine Eigenthümlichkeit der Produktion an
der Mosel, daß Werth darauf gelegt wird, die Eigenart des
Rieslingweines zu voller, ungeschmälerter Wirkung zu bringen,
und mit welchem Erfolge in dieser Richtung gearbeitet wird,
das beweisen die Preise, die in der Neuzeit für die Hochgewächse der Mosel angelegt werden. In den Preisen haben
sich die besten Weine der Mosel denen des Rheines sehr ge-
nähert, nicht in der Qualität. Mosel bleibt Mosel. In der
Entfaltung der einzigartigen, kostbaren Besonderheit des Moselweines ist der Zauber zu suchen, mit welchem Schritt für
Schritt die Gunst des Publikums erobert wird.

Es gibt nur einen Moselwein. Groß sind die Unter-
schiede in der Qualität, denn die Spanne von $M.$ 400 bis
$M.$ 12 750 für das Fuder ist weit, und es findet sich für jede
Zwischenstufe die rechte Sorte, aber es gehört doch alles zu
ein und derselben Weinfamilie. Art läßt nicht von Art. Auch
die kleineren Weine zeigen deutlich, daß sie von Moseltrauben
stammen, und gar manches Fuder ist unter ihnen, dessen
Eigenschaften ahnen lassen, zu welch herrlicher Pracht die
Moselrasse in den besseren und besten Gewächsen sich entwickelt.
Zu den Moselweinen zählen alle von Trier abwärts wachsenden
und außerdem die Weine der unteren Saar. Darüber an
einer anderen Stelle mehr.

Eine Klassifikation nach den Produktionsorten ist nicht angängig. Es ist nicht alles erste Sorte, was in den Piesporter Weinbergen oder im großen Brauneberg oder in Oberemmel u. s. w. wächst. Man könnte nur die einzelnen Weinbergslagen in eine Rangordnung bringen, wofür die an der Mosel zur Veranlagung der Grundsteuer eingeführte Bonitirung nach acht Klassen eine verwendbare Grundlage abgeben würde, aber es wäre eine Riesenarbeit zu bewältigen, ohne daß man zu einer verwerthbaren Uebersicht käme. Es sind jedoch folgende allgemeine Angaben möglich.

Erste Qualitäten: Die besten Gewächse vom Scharzhofberg, vom Bockstein und Geisberg, vom Agritiusberg, Rosenberg und aus der Lage Raul an der Saar; von Piesport, vom Brauneberg, von Bernkastel (Doktor), vom Josefshof, vom Zeltinger Schloßberg an der Mosel. Seit dem merkwürdigen Resultate mit dem Jahrgang 1893 gehören auch die Maximiner Grünhäuser Herrenberger von der Ruwer hierher.

Daran schließen sich andere Gewächse von genannten Stellen an und außerdem solche, in der Thalrichtung von oben nach unten, a) an der Saar: Ayler, Scharzberger, Canzemer, Wawerner Herrenberger; b) an der Mosel: Thiergärtner, Avelsbacher, Augenscheiner, Caseler, Mertesdorfer, Karthäuserhofberger (die letzten 3 im Ruwerthale), Neumagener, Throner, Minheimer, Ohligsberger, Neuberger, Geierslay, Paulinsberger, Elisenberger, Niederberger, Graacher, Wehlener, Zeltinger, Uerziger, Erdener, Lösenicher, Kinheimer, Trarbacher, Trabener, Enkircher. Dann kommen die übrigen Weine der Mittelmosel sowie die der Untermosel, wo sich noch Cochem, Cobern und Winningen durch Produktion besserer Qualitäten auszeichnen.

Daß die Moselweine erst in der Neuzeit so recht zu Ehre und Ansehen gekommen sind, hat wohl hauptsächlich seinen Grund in der ehemaligen mangelhaften Zugänglichkeit des Gebietes. Bis in die zweite Hälfte dieses Jahrhunderts war das Moselgebiet für seinen Verkehr mit der übrigen Welt auf den Wasserweg angewiesen. Erst dann erfolgte der Bau der

Mosellandstraße, anfangs von Coblenz bis Alf und später über Zell, Trarbach und Bernkastel weiter. Im Jahre 1879 wurde der Betrieb der Trier mit Coblenz verbindenden Mosel- eisenbahn eröffnet, und erst seit dieser Zeit kann das Gebiet als richtig aufgeschlossen gelten.

Ein nicht zahlreicher aber sehr rühriger Weinhandel an der Mosel hat sich schnell in die veränderte Situation hinein- gefunden, und er hat es verstanden, in kurzer Frist mit einem beispiellosen Erfolge die Moselweine in den großen Verkehr einzuführen. Es waren hauptsächlich die kleineren und mittleren Qualitäten, mit welchen die Bahn gebrochen wurde. Aber auch die Produktion blieb nicht zurück. Auf die Resultate der nebenbei gesagt mit vielem Geschick arrangirten großen Trierer Weinversteigerungen hat in den Jahren 1895, 1896 und 1897 alle Welt mit Staunen geblickt. Heute strahlt der Glanz, mit welchem sich die feinen Moselweine umgeben haben, zurück auch auf die geringeren Qualitäten, und so steht gegenwärtig alles in schönster Wechselwirkung. Die kleinen Weine helfen den feinen und die feinen den kleinen, und dabei gehen Produktion und Handel, welche sich offen zur Solidarität ihrer Interessen bekennen, einträchtig Hand in Hand. An der Mosel selbst — von Trier bis Coblenz — mag es etwa 80 Weinhandlungen geben, welche das Geschäft im großen betreiben, und eine etwas größere Zahl von Handlungen, welche direkt mit dem Konsum arbeiten. Haupt- weinhandelsplätze sind: Trier, Dusemond, Mülheim, Cues, Bernkastel, Zeltingen, Trarbach-Traben, Zell, Merl, Cochem- Cond, Winningen und Coblenz. Außerhalb des Moselgebietes hat Cöln bedeutenden Moselweinhandel.

Der Moselwein wird seinen Weg weiter machen. „Er lockelt“, heißt es an der Mosel in launigem Provinzialismus, d. h. er lockt, er reizt zum Weitertrinken. Er ist auch in der That der Kneipwein wie er im Buche steht. Und wer des Moselweins Gefunkel mit etwas poetischen Augen anzu- schauen versteht, dem lacht aus dem lichten, grüngoldigen Naß die frische Ursprünglichkeit des Lebens an der Mosel entgegen, die märchenhafte Romantik des Thales schimmert hervor, und all das Sonnenfeuer, das die Traube gezeitigt, sprüht neu auf im krystallenen Glase.

Nun putzt die Gläser blitzeblank,
Es kommt der rechte Tropfen!
Und unter lautem Sang und Klang
Ziehn wir den ersten Stopfen.
    Der Wein ist deutsch, der Wein ist gut,
    Ist echtes Moselrebenblut.

Er ist nicht voll und dick und schwer
Und auch nicht plump und stuftig;
Er hat die allerfeinste Gähr,
Ist wie ein Röslein duftig.
    Der Wein ist deutsch, der Wein ist gut,
    Ist echtes Moselrebenblut.

So freudig wie die Sonne strahlt
Ins Moselthal hernieder,
Und wenn man sonst auch noch so prahlt,
Das gibt's ja gar nicht wieder.
    Der Wein ist deutsch, der Wein ist gut,
    Ist echtes Moselrebenblut.

Und fröhlich baut im Sonnenbrand
Der Winzer seine Reben,
Weil lustig wird des Zechers Hand
Das Moselglas erheben.
    Der Wein ist deutsch, der Wein ist gut,
    Ist echtes Moselrebenblut.

So plagt uns gar kein Herzeleid,
Wir müssen weiter trinken,
Und sollten wir vor Seligkeit
Uns in die Arme sinken.
    Der Wein ist deutsch, der Wein ist gut,
    Ist echtes Moselrebenblut.

Das Weinbaugebiet der Mosel.

———◇———

Auf sonn'ger Bergesseite,
  Da steh'n die Reben schlank;
In tiefer Keller=Weite,
  Da liegt manch kühler Trank.
      O lichter Schein;
      O kühler Wein!
Ihr grünen Berge, o Fluß und Thal,
Ich grüß' euch von Herzen viel tausendmal.

Aus dem Mosellied von Neck.

Die Mosel ist so recht ein Weinfluß, von oben bis unten.
Schon unweit des Quellgebietes auf französischem Boden be=
ginnt der Weinbau, der als treuer Begleiter dem Fluß zur
Seite bleibt, bis dessen Fluthen sich einen mit den grünen
Wellen des Rheines.

Ungefähr eine Meile unterhalb des Städtchens Pont à
Mousson erreicht die Mosel die deutsche Grenze, folgt dieser
eine kurze Strecke, und tritt dann in der Nähe von Novéant
ganz in das Reichsland Lothringen ein, welches sie zwischen
Sierck und Perl wieder verläßt. Nunmehr als Grenzfluß
zwischen Luxemburg und Deutschland dahinströmend, wendet
sie sich bei Wasserbillig — nicht weit von Trier — in die
Rheinprovinz, um hier jenes merkwürdige Weinthal zu durch=
messen, auf welches der preußische Rheinländer fast stolzer ist,
als auf seinen Rhein.

Aus den Neumagener Skulpturen.
Weinschiff.

Im französischen Moselgebiet herrscht die Produktion des Roth= weines, des Nationalgetränkes der Franzosen, vor, und auch Deutsch= Lothringen verdankt seinen Ruf als Weinland dem Anbau von rothen Sorten, deren beste Qualitäten, zu Claret gekeltert, gegenwärtig als sehr begehrter Stoff zur Herstellung von Schaumwein in die deutschen Sektkellereien wandern. Im lothringischen Kreise Diedenhofen hört der Rothweinbau auf.

Daselbst fängt der Weißweinbau an, der nunmehr der Mosel in ihrem gan= zen ferneren Laufe eigenthümlich bleibt und weiter unten zwischen Trier und Coblenz jenes ras= sige Produkt liefert, den eigentlichen Mo= selwein, welcher mit einem Erfolge ohne=

Aus den Neumagener Skulpturen
Rebenornament.

gleichen gegenwärtig mitten in seinem Siegeszuge durch die deutschen Gauen und darüber hinaus begriffen ist.

Aus den Neumagener Skulpturen.
Weinschiff.

Schon in Lothringen spricht man von einem oberen und einem unteren Mosellaufe und man nimmt die Mündung der Orne in die Mo= sel als die Grenze zwischen beiden an. Aber in der preußischen Rhein= provinz theilt man anders ein. Was von oben bis zur Saarmün= dung in der Nähe von Trier reicht, gilt als Obermosel, dann folgt die Mittelmosel bis etwa in die Gegend von Cochem, und endlich von hier bis Coblenz die Untermosel. Rein geographischen Anforderungen entspricht weder die eine noch die andere Eintheilung des Flußlaufes, die des=wegen beide nur einen lokalen Charakter tragen. In der Rheinprovinz spielt dabei vielleicht gerade der Weinbau eine Rolle, und es ist allemal in dem Sinne der hierselbst land=läufigen Eintheilung, wenn in diesem Büchlein von Obermosel, Mittelmosel und Untermosel die Rede ist.

Das Thal der Mittel= und Untermosel schneidet tief ein zwischen rauhem Hochland links, der Eifel, und rauhem Hoch=land rechts, dem Hunsrück, im allgemeinen in der Richtung von Südwest nach Nordost. Bald nach der einen, bald nach der anderen Seite ausweichend, windet sich die Mosel durch die felsigen Abhänge hindurch.

> Was krümmt die Mosel sich so sehr?
> O weh, sie muß zum Rhein, zum Meer,
> Und möcht daheim nur sein, und möcht daheim nur sein.
>
> Theobald Kerner.

Welchem Moselkind in der Fremde greift bei diesen tief empfundenen Worten nicht das Heimweh ans Herz! Daheim! Daheim im Märchenlande der Mosel, unten der blinkende Spiegel des Flusses, oben auf den steilen Hängen die alte Burg, dazwischen das frische Grün der Reben, und alles über=strahlt vom klarblauen Himmel!

Jäh stürzt das Hochland auf beiden Seiten nach der Mosel ab, und wo der Fluß in den zahlreichen Krümmungen von der allgemeinen Südwest=Nordost=Richtung abweicht, da schiebt sich die Schieferwand des Ufers quer in die Strahlen der Sonne hinein, bereit, das Sonnenkind, die Rebe, in den nährenden Boden aufzunehmen. Den Windungen des Thales verdankt die Mosel jene bald auf der rechten, bald auf der linken Seite nach Süden abfallenden Uferränder, welche zum Weinbau geradezu prädestinirt erscheinen.

Ruinen des röm. Amphitheaters
bei Trier.

Ruinen des römischen Kaiserpalastes
in Trier.

Man hat schon früh
erkannt, daß die Kultur
der Rebe in das für sie
wie geschaffene Moselthal
hineingehöre. Bekanntlich
besingt der lateinische Dichter Ausonius in seiner „Mosella",
der berühmten Idylle, den blühenden Weinbau an der Mosel,
wie er ihn gelegentlich einer Reise im Jahre 370 n. Chr.
mit eigenen Augen geschaut hatte. Man glaubte ehedem,
daß der römische Kaiser Probus (276 bis 282 n. Chr.)
den Weinbau dahin gebracht habe. Diese Anschauung er=
litt einen schweren Stoß, als vor einigen Jahren die merk=
würdigen Funde von Neumagen gemacht wurden. Unter den
zahlreichen Skulpturen, welche damals ausgegraben wurden und
jetzt im Museum zu Trier aufbewahrt werden, sind manche,
welche beweisen, daß schon in der ersten Hälfte des zweiten
Jahrhunderts unserer Zeitrechnung an der Mosel Wein=
handel sich entwickelt hatte, und welche vermuthen lassen,
daß zu gleicher Zeit auch Weinbau daselbst vorhanden war.
Hochinteressant sind die verschiedenen Bruchstücke der mit Wein=
fässern beladenen Schiffe und von nicht minderer Bedeutung

ift ein großer Quader, deſſen eine Fläche mit Rebenornament
bedeckt iſt. Im Schnitt der Rebe auf dem Stein iſt eine
gewiſſe Aehnlichkeit mit der heute noch an der Moſel üblichen
Rebenzuchtmethode unverkennbar. Ich habe im Herbſt 1894
beim Weinbaukongreß in Mainz des näheren ausgeführt,
wie aus den Funden von Neumagen und aus anderen
Umſtänden der Schluß zu ziehen iſt, daß lange vor der Zeit,
in welcher die Neumagener Skulpturen angefertigt wurden, der
Weinbau an die Moſel gelangte und zwar vermuthlich nicht
durch die Römer, ſondern durch die daſelbſt anſäſſigen Tre-
virer, jenes merkwürdige, mächtige Volk, das häufig zu
den Kelten gezählt wird, obgleich es ſelbſt, wie Tacitus in
ſeiner Germania bezeugt, ſich ſeiner germaniſchen Abſtammung
eifrig berühmte.

Wie oft mögen in der ſpätrömiſchen Kaiſerzeit im Kaiſer-
palaſt von Auguſta Trevirorum, deſſen maleriſche Ruinen
heute zu den Hauptſehenswürdigkeiten Triers zählen, die
ministri vini die calices (calix = Kelch) mit Moſelwein
gefüllt haben, wenn ein Trinkgelage dem Gaſtmahl als Spitze
folgte! Ob auch wohl damals das rieſige Amphitheater, deſſen
Reſte heute an dem Abhange eines Weinberges liegen, zwiſchen
Reben eingebettet war?

Der römiſchen Kaiſerherrlichkeit folgte der Sturm der
Völkerwanderung, der vielleicht die Weinberge vom Boden
wegfegte. Aber die Unterbrechung des Weinbaues kann nicht
lange gedauert haben. Er ſtand bereits zu Beginn der Franken-
zeit, als die Völker ſeßhaft geworden waren, bei den ripuariſchen
Franken an der Moſel unter geſetzlichem Schutz. Nach der
intereſſanten Zuſammenſtellung von Karl Reichelt (Reut-
lingen 1886) iſt der Weinbau an der Moſel urkundlich zuerſt
belegt aus dem Jahre 634, wo König Dagobert dem Erz-
biſchof Modoald zu Trier alle Rechte und Güter ſeiner Kirche
beſtätigte, darunter auch Weinberge am Rhein, an der Loire
und an der Moſel. Für einzelne Ortſchaften in den
Regierungsbezirken Trier und Coblenz iſt — ebenfalls nach

Reichelt — der Weinbau urkundlich nachgewiesen aus Jahren des siebenten, achten, neunten und zehnten Jahrhunderts. Im Jahre 1000, in welchem der Weinbau überhaupt in Deutsch= land schon sehr ausgedehnt war, mag bereits das ganze Thal der mittleren und unteren Mosel ein zusammenhängendes Weinland gewesen sein. So ist es auch noch heute, wo von

Trier bis Coblenz in fast ununterbro= chener Folge sich ein Weinberg an den andern reiht.

Es sind echte, rechte Weinberge, welche die Mosel säumen. Sie ver= fehlen nicht des Eindrucks als sol= che auf den Nicht= weinländer, der sich den ihm unbekann= ten Weinbau als in steiler Berglage erfolgend vorstellt und immer mit einer gewissen Ent=

Stationsbild in den Weinbergen bei Cond.

täuschung dessen Bekanntschaft macht, wenn er zuerst flache oder flachhügelige Lagen sieht. So jählings steigt oft an der Mosel der Berghang in die Höhe, daß durch einen kunst= vollen Terrassenbau die Böschung gemäßigt werden muß, damit die Rebe eingesetzt und gepflegt werden kann. Gar malerisch ist das Bild, wenn der Weinbau an der kantigen Klippe Terrasse um Terrasse hinaufklimmt, hier mit einem Wein= bergshüttchen in den Reben, dort mit einem Stationshäuschen an der Wegecke, wie man solche zu Wallfahrtszwecken in die Weinberge eingestreut findet.

Mühsam ist der Rebenbau in den steilen Lagen. Der Winzer muß nicht allein seine Person mit seinen eigenen Beinen hinaufbefördern, er muß auch alles, was der Rebe nöthig ist, nach oben schleppen, ob die Sonne mitten in den Weinberg hineinbrennt oder ob im Winter der eisige Ostwind vom Hunsrück herüberpfeift. Läge für den Winzer nicht ein verklärender Zauber im Rebenbau, es könnte schier zu viel werden! Ein Abglanz der Poesie des Weines überstrahlt auch den Weinbau; ihn kann und will der Winzer nicht missen, sei das Weinjahr ein gutes, oder sei es ein schlechtes.

Und es gibt so viele der kleinen Winzer, deren freudig pflegender Hand die Rebe bedarf, sowohl in ihren eigenen Weinbergen als auch in denen der großen Güter, für welche sie die Arbeit schaffen. Wohl nirgendwoanders im deutschen Weinlande ist der Rebenbau so sehr die Domäne des kleinen Mannes wie an der Mosel, nirgendwoanders ist die Parzellirung des Besitzes eine so entwickelte. Im Durchschnitt kommen an der Mosel auf den einzelnen Besitzer 15 Parzellen, z. B. in Piesport 20, in Lieser 26, in Merl 30 und in Wolf sogar 45 Parzellen. Eine Folge dieser Parzellirung ist der Umstand, daß man die Weinberge nach einer sehr kleinen Maßeinheit kauft, früher nach der Quadratruthe, und jetzt häufig nach dem Quadratmeter oder nach dem Stock. Es kommt vor, daß der einzelne Stock in guten Lagen mit zwanzig Mark und mehr bezahlt wird, während er in den geringsten Lagen nicht höher als 70 Pfennig zu stehen kommt.

Mit 2000 bis 2500 Stöcken ist der Morgen von 2500 Quadratmeter bestanden. Die guten Lagen sind weniger dicht bestockt, mit 2000 Stöcken auf den Morgen; die mittleren etwas dichter, mit ungefähr 2250 Stöcken; und die geringeren am dichtesten, mit 2500 Stöcken, mitunter vielleicht noch etwas mehr.

Es gibt an der mittleren und unteren Mosel — also die obere Mosel gar nicht mitgerechnet — im ganzen mehr als 22 600 Morgen Weinberge, auf welchen im Durchschnitt

Weinbergsterrassen am Pinneberg bei Cochem.

einer größeren Reihe von Jahren etwa
16 000 bis 17 000 Fuder Wein, das
Fuder von 975 Liter, jährlich erzielt
werden. Der Ertrag ist je nach der
Ergiebigkeit des Jahres außerordent=
lich verschieden. Es kommen Miß=
jahre vor, in welchen der Morgen
nicht mehr als ein einziges Hektoliter
liefert, während ein voller Herbst zwei
Fuder vom Morgen bringen kann.

Zur Unsicherheit inbezug auf das Quantum gesellt sich noch die Unsicherheit inbezug auf die Qualität, so daß der Erfolg des Weinbaues stets ein sehr zweifelhafter ist. Reihen sich mehrere Fehljahre an einander, wie es leider vorkommt, dann bricht für den kleinen Winzer die Zeit der schweren Noth an. Das war früher, als Handel und Verkehr nicht so entwickelt waren, noch schlimmer als jetzt. Aber sehr empfindlich ist es

Burg Eltz.

auch heute noch, und so groß die Anhänglichkeit an die Reben auch sein mag, und so hoch die Hoffnung auf bessere Zeiten gehalten werden mag, so genügt das doch nicht, des Lebens Nothdurft zu befriedigen. Es ist noch eines, was dem Winzer hilft, den Kopf oben zu behalten: Der Gedanke, daß gerade der Weinbau für den kleinen Mann besser paßt als irgend ein anderer landwirthschaftlicher Erwerbszweig, daß er dem Winzer Gelegenheit gibt, mitsammt seiner Familie gewissermaßen bei sich selbst im Tagelohn zu arbeiten und zwar in der freien Gotteswelt, was doch immer noch besser ist, als sein Brod

2

Der alte Zollthurm in Trarbach.

im dumpfstaubigen Fabriksaale zu verdienen. Schätze lassen sich beim Weinbau nicht sammeln, und darauf rechnet der Winzer auch gar nicht. Aber stolz ist und bleibt er auf seine Reben, möge das Jahr ein ganzes Füllhorn reichen Erntesegens über ihn ausschütten oder möge es schwere Enttäuschung bringen.

Von den an der Mosel angebauten Traubensorten ist in erster Linie der Riesling zu nennen, die im Rheinland heimische edelste Bouquettraube der ganzen Welt. Wie die Mosel, so will auch sie d a h e i m sein. Sie bedarf des heimischen Bodens, um die herrliche Pracht ihres Produktes zur vollen Entfaltung zu bringen. Der Thonschiefer der Berghänge, auf dem fast sämmtliche Reben der Mittel- und der Untermosel stehen, sagt ihr ganz besonders zu; aus ihm saugt sie die unwägbaren Stoffe, welche dem Moselwein die köstliche Eigenart aufprägen. Draußen im fremden Land, wo man ebenfalls solch ein Juwel besitzen möchte und wo man schon oft Versuche mit ihrem Anbau machte, entartet sie.

In zweiter Linie steht die Kleinberger Rebe, auch Elben oder Elbling genannt, die ehemals sogar vor dem Riesling vorherrschte. Sie liefert einen festen, rassigen Wein, der aber an das Aroma und das Bouquet des Rieslingweines nicht heranreicht. Abgesehen vom Heunisch, der auf dem Kalkboden der oberen Mosel den Hauptbestand des Rebensatzes bildet, kommen andere Sorten nur vereinzelt vor. Sie spielen keine Rolle. Rothweine werden nur an wenigen Stellen produzirt.

Mit dem poetischen Zauber des Weinbaues eint sich im Moselthale der fesselnde Reiz der mittelalterlichen Romantik, um so ein wunderbares Märchenland zu schaffen, das seinesgleichen sucht. Die Trümmer von zahlreichen Burgen krönen malerischer, als es die lebhafte Phantasie eines Künstlers sich ausdenken könnte, die Höhen, und hie und da ist auch ein Stück in

Blick vom Hospital Cues
nach Bernkastel.

seinem alten Glanze ganz erhalten geblieben. Wie schauen alle die Ecken und Kanten der Kultur des Mittelalters aus den Thürmchen, den Erkern und den wie Schwalbennester angeklebten Gelassen der berühmten Burg Elz hervor, ohne welche ein echtes Moselkind sich das heimische Land gar nicht zu denken vermag! Kann es für die schwerfällige Tüchtigkeit des Bürgerthums vergangener Zeiten — für die Deftigkeit desselben, wenn ich hier die Sprache des Volkes reden darf, die den Nagel allemal auf den Kopf trifft, — einen sprechenderen Zeugen geben als den massigen, untersetzten Bau des alten Zollthurmes in Trarbach? Und wenn man ein echtes Mosel=

2*

landschaftsbild sehen will, wenn man verstehen will, wie auf
dem Fetzen ebenen Geländes zwischen Fluß und Berghang die
Ortschaft sich aufbaut und an die Falten des letzteren sich an-
klammert, so wende man das Auge nach einer Perle der
Mosel wie z. B. Bernkastel.

An der mittleren Mosel ist der Weinbau intensiver als
an der unteren. Dort drängen sich auch die besseren Lagen
mehr aneinander, die hier nur vereinzelt auftreten. Genau
läßt sich die Grenze zwischen Mittel- und Untermosel nicht
angeben. Die einen suchen sie bei Trarbach-Traben, da, wo
der Regierungsbezirk Trier sich vom Regierungsbezirk Coblenz
scheidet, andere etwas weiter unten in der Gegend von Alf,
und wieder andere bei Cochem. Zwischen Trier und Cochem
hat vorzugsweise die Mosel jene oben erwähnten Krümmungen,
welche für den Weinbau von besonderem Segen sind, während
unterhalb Cochems die Mosel in mehr geradegerichtetem Laufe
Coblenz zueilt. Ich glaube, daß diejenigen, welche die Grenze
bei Cochem annehmen, recht haben.

Die Weine der oberen Mosel kommen als eigentliche
Moselweine nicht in Betracht; sie bilden eine Sorte für sich.
Ueber die Weinorte der mittleren Mosel, wohin auch die der
unteren Saar gehören, und die der unteren Mosel im folgenden Kapitel nun noch einige Details.

Die Weinorte der Mosel.

———⁂———

Ich höre Winzersang,
Der Waldbach rauscht, die Burgen nah'n,
Schon tanzt den Fluß entlang,
Von Dorf zu Dorf mein Kahn.
      Trinkt und singt!
Der Becher perlt von Moselwein,
Und wo sein Klang erklingt,
Da fällt mein Anker ein.

Pfarrius.

Obschon es, wie bereits gesagt, nur e i n e n Moselwein gibt, so thut man doch gut, sein langgedehntes Produktionsgebiet in verschiedene Strecken einzutheilen, wenn man es besser übersehen will. Die in der Rheinprovinz gültige lokalgeographische Unterscheidung zwischen Mittelmosel und Untermosel wird auch gern in weinbaulicher Beziehung gebraucht. Sowohl nach der Menge als auch nach der Güte der erzeugten Weine hat die mittlere Mosel vor der unteren den Vorrang. Nun kann man wohl das Produktionsgebiet der Untermosel in einem Stücke gut überblicken, jedoch nicht so das der Mittelmosel, das man deswegen besser in weinbaulich unterschiedene Bezirke abgrenzt. Da das Saargebiet zur mittleren Mosel zählt, so ist zunächst dieses abzusondern und dann das Thal der Mittelmosel bei Piesport in zwei Strecken zu trennen. Es ergibt sich nunmehr folgende Eintheilung:

1. Das Saargebiet; 2. Die Mosel von der Saarmündung bis Piesport; 3. Die Mosel von Piesport bis Cochem; 4. Die Mosel von Cochem bis Coblenz.

Das Saargebiet.

Bei Conz ergießt sich die Saar in die Mosel. Der Mündungswinkel auf der rechten Seite der Saar, wo nur die Weinberge von Conz als Mosellagen gelten, ist hauptsächlich das Produktionsgebiet der Saarweine. Denkt man sich denselben durch eine Linie von Saarburg nach Trier abgezogen, so bezeichnet das Dreieck zwischen Saarburg, Conz und Trier annähernd jenes gesegnete Fleckchen Erde, auf welchem die hochberühmten Saarweine reifen. Der Weinbau greift nur wenig über die Linie Saarburg — Conz auf das linke Saarufer hinüber. Klein ist das Gebiet und nicht zahlreich sind die Ortschaften, welche die Rebe kultiviren, aber sie haben es wahrlich verstanden, von sich reden zu machen.

Die Summe dieser Saarweinberge beträgt ungefähr 490 Hektar = 1960 Morgen, auf welchen jährlich im Durchschnitt etwa 1500 Fuder Wein wachsen. Die Saarproduktion partizipirt also am Gesammtweinbau des Gebietes der mittleren und unteren Mosel annähernd mit nur einem Zehntel, aber ihre Bedeutung als Qualitätsbau wird sofort klar, wenn man ihre Betheiligung an den großen Trierer Weinversteigerungen feststellt. Vom Jahrgange 1893 wurden z. B. in Trier im ganzen 1567½ Fuder versteigert. Davon entfielen allein 646½ Fuder auf die Saarweine, welche durchschnittlich $\mathcal{M}$. 3547 für das Fuder erlösten, während die übrigen 921 Fuder es auf durchschnittlich $\mathcal{M}$. 2946 brachten.

Den Saarweinen rühmt man allgemein nach, daß sie das edle Rieslingbouquet noch etwas ausgesprochener zeigen als die Weine aus dem Moselthale. Sie sind auch noch dünner, flüchtiger und ferner wohl noch lichter von Farbe als diese, sonst jedoch im allgemeinen von echtem Moselcharakter.

Wie das ganze Saarthal eine gewisse Aehnlichkeit mit dem Moselthale zeigt mit einer Abtönung nach dem Lieblichen hin, so erfolgt der Weinbau daselbst in weniger steilen Lagen. Es sind sanfter geneigte Hänge, an welchen die Rebe gedeiht, und sie liegen meistens nicht unmittelbar an der Saar, sondern in Seitenthälern. Auch darin unterscheidet sich der

Der Scharzhof.

Weinbau der Saar von dem der Mosel, daß an jener die Zersplitterung des Rebenbesitzes nicht vorherrscht wie an dieser. Die Weinberge an der Saar sind mehr in der Hand von Großproduzenten.

In der Richtung des Saarthales von oben nach unten reihen sich in diesem Gebiete die Weinorte wie folgt an einander:

Staadt bei Saarburg links; die gute Lage Saarstein der Gemeinde Serrig rechts; Saarburg links; Beurig und Irsch rechts; Niederleuken links; Ockfen, wo jetzt auch der Staat Weinberge angelegt hat, rechts, in der Nähe die vortrefflichen Lagen Bockstein und Geisberg; Ayl links, etwas zurückliegend, mit der guten Lage Neuberg; Biebelshausen links; Schoden rechts; Wiltingen rechts, in der Nähe die berühmten Lagen Scharzhofberg und Scharzberg; Canzem links mit den Weinbergen auf der rechten Seite, darunter die gute Lage Kelterberg; Wawern links, etwas zurückliegend, mit der ausgezeichneten Lage Herrenberg; Hamm rechts, Filzen rechts. Den Schluß macht links Cönen, wo ein beliebter Rothwein gebaut wird.

Sehr wichtig ist dann noch das östlich von Wiltingen ziehende sogenannte Oberemmelerthal. Breit furcht die Thalmulde das Land, nach der Vermuthung des Landesgeologen Grebe das alte Bett eines Moselarms, der in der Urzeit daselbst geströmt haben soll. Hierher gehören die Orte Oberemmel mit den berühmten Lagen Rosenberg, Agritiusberg (an der Kirche), Raul, Lautersberg, Junkerberg; Crettnach; Ober- und Niedermennig mit den vorzüglichen Lagen Euchariusberg und Zuckerberg.

Wiltingen hat mit ca. 400 Morgen den ausgedehntesten Weinbau; dann folgen Oberemmel mit ca. 280 Morgen;

Dorfeingang
in Oberemmel.

Ochsen mit 160 Morgen; Canzem mit ca. 150 Morgen; Ayl und Wawern mit je ca. 120 Morgen; sowie die übrigen Gemarkungen je mit einer Weinbaufläche unter 120 Morgen.

Von den genannten besten Weinbergslagen haben sich die meisten einen solchen Namen gemacht, daß sie ganz für sich allein, ohne Beifügung des Gemarkungsnamens, die Reise durch die Welt unternehmen können.

Die Mosel von der Saarmündung bis Piesport.

Ungefähr auf halbem Wege von der Saarmündung bis Piesport versteckt sich hinter einem Wald von Apfelbäumen der große, behäbige Weinort Schweich als Pförtner des engen Moselthales, das von hier an scharf eingeschnitten in das rheinische Schiefergebirge sich in den zahlreichen für den Mosellauf so charakteristischen Krümmungen hinzieht zum Rheine.

Aber von Schweich an aufwärts dehnt und streckt sich das
Thal bis zur Saar, etwa 3 Kilometer breit und 20 lang, und
fast gerade aus der Mitte der üppigen Gefilde der Thalebene
grüßen die Thürme von Trier heraus. Man nennt dieses
Stück der Mosel wohl das Trierer Thal, das sich von der
Kirche bei Conz bis Schweich, also seiner ganzen Länge nach,
überschauen läßt. Aber schöner zeigen sich auf= und abwärts

Das Grünhaus.

die Herrlichkeiten, wenn man von der schroffen Felsenkante bei
Pallien, Trier gerade gegenüber, Auslug hält.

So verschieden das landschaftliche Gepräge des Trierer
Thales einerseits und des Moselthales unterhalb Schweichs
andererseits, so verschieden ist auch dort und hier der wein=
bauliche Charakter. Hier im Moselthale bedrängen dicht am
Wasser die Weinberge den Fluß, dort im Trierer Thale ziehen
sie sich dagegen vom Uferrand mehr zurück.

Oberhalb Schweichs ist auf dem linken Ufer der Wein=
bau unbedeutend. Es sind nur die zwei Lagen Irminen und
Augenschein bei Trier zu nennen, von welchen die letztgenannte
ausnahmsweise scharf an die Mosel heranrückt. Sie soll ihren
Namen daher haben, daß sie den Mönchen des gegenüber
liegenden Klosters St. Marien besonders in die Augen stach.
Auf dem rechten Ufer hat Conz nicht unbedeutenden Wein=
bau und dann kommt gleich der Stadtkreis Trier mit

faſt 500 Morgen Weinbergen. Hier wachſen bei O l e w i g
bezw. K ü r e n z die berühmten Thiergärtner und Avels=
bacher. Auch die Lagen Pichter und Neuberg gehören zu
den beſſeren.

Nicht weit von Trier mündet rechts bei R u w e r die Ruwer
in die Moſel. Sie hat hervorragenden Weinbau, der oben bei
W a l d r a c h beginnt und ſich über C a ſ e l und M e r t e s d o r f
fortſetzt nach E i t e l s b a c h, bei welchem Orte rechts der Kar=
thäuſerhof und links das Grünhaus gelegen. Die Caſeler,
Karthäuſerhofberger und Grünhäuſer ſind Sterne in der langen
Reihe der Moſelweinnamen von Ruf, und zwei Fuder 1893er
Maximiner Grünhäuſer Herrenberger haben ſich bei den Trierer
Frühjahrsweinverſteigerungen von 1896 den Ruhm erworben,
mit *M.* 11010 bezw. *M.* 12750 die höchſten Preiſe erzielt
zu haben, welche je für Moſelweine angelegt wurden. Das
Grünhaus, das früher ad valles hieß, wurde von König
Dagobert I. der Abtei St. Maximin geſchenkt, was am 7. Januar
966 von Otto I. beſtätigt wurde. Dabei war ausgehalten,

Der Karthäuſerhof.

daß am erſten jeden
Monats für den
König gebetet werde,
und daß dann die
Mönche einen tüch=
tigen Zug Grün=
häuſer thun ſollten.
Merkwürdiger Wei=
ſe nennt man die
Weine des Ruwer=
thales „Heckenweine." Das Thal iſt gut aufgeſchloſſen durch
die Eiſenbahn nach Hermeskeil.

Zwiſchen der Ruwer und der Moſel unterhalb Schweichs
haben noch Weinbau: K e n n, F a ſ t r a u, N i e d e r f e l l und
O b e r f e l l.

Bei S c h w e i c h wechſelt plötzlich die Scenerie. Das Thal
ſchließt ſich enge zuſammen, die Weinberge treten auf der linken

Seite dicht an die Mosel heran und begleiten diese über Longuich, das aber rechts, also den Weinbergen gegenüber liegt, sodann weiter über Longen, Lörsch und Mehring bis Pölich. Bei Longuich bedecken die Reben den Abhang des hohen Schückberges, dessen Gipfel früher als Hexentanzplatz berüchtigt war, heute aber als Aussichtspunkt berühmt ist. Rechts Riol. Gegenüber dem nach der großen Feuersbrunst vom 8. Juni 1840 neu aufgebauten Mehring klettert bei Kühstantinopel, wie der Volkswitz die zu den Weideplätzen gehörigen Gebäude getauft hat, die uralte nach Birkenfeld führende Weinstraße den Berg hinauf.

Zwischen Pölich und Schleich springt der Weinbau auf das rechte Ufer über, bleibt hier bis Detzem, um bei Ensch wieder auf die linke Seite zu gehen und hier über Thörnich, welches auf der anderen Seite liegt, das wegen seiner Länge sprichwörtlich gewordene Clüsserath zu erreichen, das viel Wein produziert. Es kommen Köwerich rechts aber die Weinberge links, und Leiwen rechts mit Weinbau auf beiden Seiten, die besten Lagen links. Gegenüber der Laurentiusberg, dessen Reben meistens Trittenheimer Produzenten gehören. Trittenheim, an einem scharfen Bogen der Mosel liegend, hat sowohl links als auch rechts den bedeutendsten Weinbau auf dieser Moselstrecke mit fast 400 Morgen, darunter manche gute Lage. Trittenheim ist nicht allein als Weinort berühmt, sondern auch als Geburtsstätte des Johannes Tritheim oder Trithemius, des um die Geschichtsschreibung des Mittelalters verdienten Abtes von Sponheim. „Seine Annalen haben trotz ihrer Fabeln und Unzuverlässigkeiten doch besonders viele Anekdoten aus frühern Jahrhunderten überliefert, die unserer lieben Jugend noch immer das Geschichtsstudium würzen, so die Erzählung von der Weinsberger Weibertreue" sagt von ihm der Moselschriftsteller Karl Hessel.

Auch der stattliche Ort Neumagen, dessen Häuser am Flusse aus üppigen Gärten freundlich hervorlugen, das alte Noviomagus in der Römerzeit, steckt mitten im Weinbau und hat mehrere gute Lagen. Hier gelangte die Römerstraße, von Bingen über den Hunsrück an die Mosel, und hier that der bereits erwähnte Dichter Ausonius nach seiner Reise durch die Wildniß des Soonwaldes zuerst den Blick in das Weinthal, dem er in seiner anmuthigen Idylle „Mosella“ ein unvergängliches Denkmal gesetzt hat. Hier stand auch die Feste des Kaisers Konstantin, und hier wurden jene alten Skulpturen ausgegraben, welche uns heute in stummer und doch so beredter Weise vom Moselwein vor fast zweitausend Jahren erzählen.

Den Schluß, aber einen glänzenden, machen die Weinberge im Seitenthale der Thron, die, nachdem sie die kleine

Piesport.

Thron, auch das Thrönchen genannt, aufgenommen hat, munterer als irgend ein anderer Hochwaldbach vom Gebirge herunterpoltert und bei Neumagen in die Mosel mündet. Die kleine Thron umspielt in ihrem Oberlaufe die durch die Nibelungensage verklärte Burg Throneck, von welcher die beiden „Tronegaere“ (Thronecker) stammen sollten, der grimme Hagen und sein im Thun rascher Bruder Dankwart. „Daz was von Tronege Hagene und’ auch der bruoder sîn, Dancwart, der vil snelle“ singt das Nibelungenlied. Der Throner Hofberg steht unter den Moselmarken von Ruf, und nicht unbedeutend ist der Weinbau des Dorfes T h r o n auf mehr als 300 Morgen. Thron gehörte früher zu dem

Fürstenthum Wagram von Napoleons Gnaden, das für den Marschall Berthier extra geschaffen war, aber nur ein ephemeres Dasein fristete. Bei der großen Retirade der Franzosen verkaufte Berthier die ihm von Napoleon geschenkten Throner Güter und überwies den Erlös der Staatskasse. Alle Achtung!

Im Weinbaugebiete von der Saarmündung bis Piesport, aber ohne diese Gemarkung, mit welcher die nächste Strecke beginnt, sind ca. 1050 Hektar = 4200 Morgen mit Reben bestockt, von welchen im Durchschnitt jährlich etwa 3000 Fuder Wein geerntet werden, d. h. fast ein Fünftel der ganzen Produktion an der mittleren und unteren Mosel.

Das Gebiet gravitirt nach Trier, dessen Ruhm als Weinstadt den alten Ruhm als Kaiserstadt des römischen Reiches fast überstrahlt. Mächtige Ruinen sind sprechende Zeugen von der vergangenen Kaiserpracht, aber wenn man heute durch die im Hauptbau wohlerhaltene, merkwürdige Porta nigra schreitet, dann nimmt einen nicht blos die Erinnerung an das römische Alterthum gefangen, sondern auch der Gedanke, daß durch dieses Thor der Weg aus der Stadt hinausführt in das gesegnete Weinthal der Mosel.

Trier hat eine gute Weinbauschule und einen bedeutenden Weinhandel. Seinen Ruf als Weinstadt verdankt es jedoch den großen Weinversteigerungen, auf welchen die besten Produkte der mittleren Mosel und der unteren Saar, die freihändig nicht verkauft werden, in den Verkehr kommen. Der vollständig freie Wettbewerb der Fachleute um den Besitz der Hochgewächse ist ein preisbildendes Moment von großer Zuverlässigkeit, und der Zufall spielt keine Rolle, wenn auf den Versteigerungen der Werth der Weine festgesetzt wird. Das Quantum, welches unter den Hammer kommt, ist im ganzen nicht bedeutend. Vom 1893er Jahrgang waren es, wie schon im vorigen Kapitel angegeben, nur 1567 1/2 Fuder, welche noch dazu auf zweimal — im Frühjahr 1895 und im Frühjahr 1896 — versteigert wurden. Dafür wurden aber mehr als 5 Millionen

Mark bezahlt. Nach der im Lintz'schen Verlage zu Trier erschienenen Tabelle ergab sich für die einzelnen Sorten der versteigerten 1893er folgendes Resultat:

Fuder von 975 Liter	Wachsthum	Durchschnitts= preis p. Fuder	Fuder von 975 Liter	Wachsthum	Durchschnitts= preis p. Fuder
	a) Mosel.			**b) Saar.**	
17	Augenscheiner . .	ℳ. 1753	30	Ayler	ℳ. 2942
39½	Avelsbacher . .	„ 3095	64½	Bocksteiner . . .	„ 4020
41	Bernkasteler . .	„ 3291	49	Canzemer . . .	„ 2780
15	Brauneberger . .	„ 4483	13½	Feilser	„ 3107
9	Throner Hofberger	„ 2833	22	Geisberger . .	„ 4393
29	Erdener . . .	„ 3138	141½	Oberemmelerthaler	
39½	Geiersleyer . .	„ 2497		Agritiusbgr.,Rauler,	
69	Graacher . . .	„ 2624		Rosenberger, Eucha-	
33½	Josefshöfer . .	„ 4443		riusberger ꝛc.) .	„ 3087
16	Irminer . . .	„ 846	52	Ockfener . . .	„ 3652
35	Lieserer Niederberger	„ 3045	25	Saarburger . .	„ 1236
34	Mattheiser . . .	„ 1637	46½	Scharzberger . .	„ 4047
15	Mehringer . .	„ 1439	70½	Scharzhofberger .	„ 5504
11	Olewiger . . .	„ 1665	18½	Staadter . . .	„ 2466
22	Ohligsberger . .	„ 3121	31	Wawerner . .	„ 4215
25½	Pichter . . .	„ 1455	82½	Wiltinger . . .	„ 3145
74	Piesporter . .	„ 3493	646½	Fuder durchschnittl.	ℳ. 3547
12	Thiergärtner . .	„ 4416		**c) Ruwer.**	
21	Trarbacher . .	„ 1253	83	Eitelsbacher = Kar-	
26	Trittenheimer . .	„ 2211		thäuserhofberger	„ 3391
21½	Uerziger . . .	„ 2132	80	Grünhäuser . .	„ 4041
52	Zeltinger . . .	„ 3682	100½	Caseler . . .	„ 2536
657½ Fuder durchschnittl. ℳ. 2818			263½ Fuder durchschnittl. ℳ. 3263		

Die im Frühjahr 1897 versteigerten 1895er erzielten für das Fuder a) Mosel 611 Fuder durchschnittlich ℳ. 2465; b) Saar 270 Fuder durchschnittlich ℳ. 3510; c) Ruwer 122 Fuder durchschnittlich ℳ. 2942.

Mit steigender Spannung folgen die im Versteigerungs= saale dichtgedrängten Kaufliebhaber dem Verlaufe des Aus= gebotes. Und wenn die Spitzen der Weine Preise erreichen, wie man sie bisher an der Mosel noch nicht kannte, dann bricht ein Beifallssturm los, daß die Wände dröhnen. An die Ehre hat der Produzent gedacht, nicht an schnöden Mammon, als der edle Tropfen in mühsamer Auslese gewonnen wurde. Daß es ihm gelungen ist, dem Ruhmeskranze der Mosel ein neues, frisches Reis einzuflechten, darauf ist alles so stolz, daß sich die Begeisterung im ungestümen Beifall Luft schafft.

Die Mosel von Piesport bis Cochem.

Wir sind in der Mitte des Produktionsgebietes der Mosel. Die oft zu beobachtende Erscheinung, daß in einem bestimmten Weinbaugebiete besonders die Mitte durch ihr Produkt nicht blos nach der Menge sondern auch nach der Güte hervorragt, macht sich an der Mosel in auffälliger Weise bemerkbar. Viel Wein wächst zwischen Piesport und Cochem, und die guten und besten Weinbergslagen sind in solcher Menge vorhanden, daß sie sich stellenweise förmlich zusammendrängen.

Die Gegend von Bernkastel ist das Herz der Mitte des Moselweinlandes. Wenn man von der Bernkasteler Brücke den Blick über die Mosellandschaft schweifen läßt, dann haftet zwar das Auge auf mancher berühmten Weinbergslage, aber der Ausschau sind in dem gewundenen Moselthale doch enge Schranken gezogen. Hier möchte man sich gerade in die Luft erheben können, um auszuspähen nach alle den Rebstücken, die sich von der Höhe herunter immer dichter und dichter vorschieben an den Rand des Flusses, dessen Silberband die eine Schleife an die andere reiht. Es ist, als wollte der eine Weinberg den anderen bei Seite drängen: „Gib Raum, hier mache ich die Sache besser als du!" Ueberall der regste Wetteifer, aber im ganzen Leben des Thales dreht sich alles um den Wein.

Mit den Weinbergen bei Piesport beginnt die Strecke. Fast in einem Halbkreis, der nach Süden geöffnet ist, so daß die Sonne mitten in die steilen, felsigen Lagen hineinbrennen kann, legen sich bei den Orten Piesport und Niederemmel (auch Emmel genannt), das mit Müstert und Reinsport eine Gemeinde bildet, die Weinberge, ungefähr 500 Morgen, am linken Ufer um einen Bogen der Mosel herum. Was soll man zum Ruhme der Piesporter Weine noch sagen, da sie selbst so laut und vernehmlich zu reden verstehen! Es war nicht immer so in Piesport wie jetzt. Im 18. Jahrhundert glaubte man gut daran zu thun, die edle Rieslingrebe durch eine andere zu ersetzen. Aber Schaden macht klug! Der Riesling hat sich den Platz zurückerobert, der für ihn wie geschaffen ist, und heute denkt niemand daran, daß hier eine andere Rebensorte besser thun könnte.

Zwischen Minheim links mit dem Rosenberg und Winterich rechts springen die Weinberge auf die rechte Seite über, wo besonders in der vorzüglichen Lage Ohligsberg, die ihren Namen von einer Kapelle „zum Oelberg" hat, und in der Lage Neuberg eines kleinen Seitenthales hervorragende Weine erzielt werden. Auch der Hof Geiersley mit seinen guten Weinen ist zu nennen. Ueber Kesten mit dem Paulinsberg links geht es weiter nach Monzel. Hier beginnt der Brauneberg, die Abhänge über und über mit Reben bedeckt, welche in einem guten Jahre an die 800 Fuder Wein liefern. Er reicht bis an das Flüßchen Lieser. Der weltbekannte Name Brauneberg ist der Sammelname für eine große Zahl guter Lagen. Drüben auf der anderen Seite Filzen mit Neufilzen, Dusemond und Mülheim; diesseits etwas weiter nach unten Lieser, zu welchen Orten der Brauneberg gehört. Dusemond und Mülheim haben lebhaften Weinhandel.

Die Gegend von Mülheim ist interessant. Auf der rechten Seite der Mosel Mülheim selbst, das etwas landeinwärts die gute Lage Elisenberg hat, auf der linken Seite schräg gegenüber Lieser mit dem ausgezeichneten Niederberg. Auf jeder Seite mündet ein kleines Weinthal, rechts das Veldenzer Thal, vom Hinterbach durchflossen, mit Veldenz; etwas rückwärts Burgen; links das Lieserthal mit den Nachbarorten Maring und Noviand, welche durch ihren Rothwein bekannt sind, und weiter aufwärts Osann und Platten.

An die Wein=
berge unterhalb des
Ortes Lieser schlie=
ßen sich die von
Andel und Cues,
die der letztgenann=
ten Ortschaft in be=
deutendem Umfange.
Cues hat auch Ruf
als Weinhandelsplatz.

Bernkastel
steht am linken Flügel
einer ganzen Kolonne
erster Lagen, die dicht ge=
schlossen das rechte Moselufer
bis Zeltingen besetzen. Gleich hinter
der malerischen Stadt eine der be=

Rathhaus in Bernkastel.

kanntesten und berühmtesten der ganzen Mosel: die Lage
Doktor. Wer kennt nicht die Sage vom schwerkranken Erz=
bischof von Trier, Boemund II., der sich gesund trank am
Doktorwein!

> Der Name Doktor aber blieb
> Dem Berg und Wein bis heute,
> Heut macht er Kranke noch gesund —
> Und froh gesunde Leute!

Der Doktorwein muß auch dem genesenen Boemund
gemundet haben, der es sich, als er später sein Amt nieder=
legte, vorsichtiger Weise vorher von seinem Nachfolger schwarz
auf weiß geben ließ, daß er der Fuder zwanzig aus der
Bernkasteler Kellerei mitnehmen dürfe.

Oberhalb der Stadt in den Weinbergen die Burg Lands=
hut; am Staden die alte Amtskellerei, wo der kurtrierische
Kellermeister wohnte und der Zehntwein eingelagert wurde;
auf dem Marktplatze das alterthümliche Rathhaus, in welchem
drei kostbare Pokale aus der Burg gezeigt werden.

3

Bernkastel hat wichtigen Weinhandel, eine gute Weinbau=
schule und etwa 400 Morgen Weinberge, darunter noch die
besseren Lagen Graben, Schwan, Rosenberg.

Gegenüber das bekannte Hospital Cues, nicht ein Kranken=
haus, sondern ein Asyl für alte Männer, wo der Stiftungs=
urkunde gemäß noch immer 33 Pfründner Aufnahme finden. In
der Nähe vom Hospital
der Bahnhof
der Neben=
bahn, wel=
che Bern=
kastel mit
der gro=
ßen Mo=
sel=Eisen=
bahn ver=
bindet.

Graach.

Rechts, um=
geben von
Weinbergen, folgt
Graach mit vie=
len hervorragend guten
Lagen, darunter Himmel=
reich und Kirchley. Am

Kelterhaus des Josefshofes.

Ende des Dorfes, an der zwischen Fluß und Weinbergen
hinziehenden Weinstraße der Josefshof mit seinem malerischen
Kelterhause, früher unter dem Namen Martinshof Eigen=
thum der Abtei St. Martin bei Trier, unter französischer
Herrschaft als Klostereigenthum konfiszirt und verkauft an
den um den Weinbau der Mosel hochverdienten Herrn Hain,
seit 1858 aber zum Kesselstatt'schen Majorat gehörig. Der
Weinname Josefshöfer ist heute in aller Welt Munde.

Wehlen links, den vorzüglichen Weinbergen gerade
gegenüber. Zu Anfang des 18. Jahrhunderts waren die

Weine des Erzstiftes Trier in fünf Klassen abgeschätzt, darunter ganz allein die Weine von Wehlen in Klasse eins. In Wehlen war früher auch die sogenannte Weingabelung in Gebrauch geradeso wie in manchen Orten des Rheingaues, d. h. es wurden von den Weinen Loose gebildet mit je einer besseren und einer geringeren Sorte, und für diese Loose wurde durch Unterhandlung mit den Käufern ein Mittelpreis festgesetzt.

Zeltingen rechts, mit Rachtig eine Gemeinde bildend, hat sehr bedeutenden

Weinbau auf mehr als 700 Morgen. Inbezug auf Menge des Produkts steht diese Gemarkung im ganzen Moselproduktionsgebiete obenan. Es wächst daselbst auch mancher gute Tropfen und der Schloßberger hat sich einen Platz unter den besten Moselweinen in der ersten Reihe erobert. In Zeltingen gibt es mehrere Weinhandlungen.

Zeltinger Schloßberg.

Die Weinberge ziehen sich auf dem linken Ufer nach Uerzig weiter, das einen — allerdings

Puricellisches Gährhaus in Zeltingen.

3 Km. vom Ort entfernten — Bahnhof an der großen Moselbahn hat. Recht gute Lage mit dem seltsamen Namen Krankenley.

Erden rechts mit ausgezeichneten Terrassen-Weinbergen links, darunter die nur auf Treppen zugängliche Lage Treppchen. Auch Lösenich rechts, mit guten Weinbergen links. Zwischen Kinheim und seiner Kolonie Kindel fließt die Mosel hindurch, aber die Weinberge liegen links. Bei Cröv links und Wolf rechts Weinbau auf beiden Seiten, jedoch die besten Lagen auf der linken; in Cröv auch Weinhandel.

Bei Wolf drängt der Trabener Berg die Mosel seitwärts, die nunmehr in einer nur wenig geöffneten Schleife fast den ganzen mächtigen Bergrücken umschlingt. Oben die Trümmer der unter Ludwig XIV. 1686 von den Franzosen erbauten Festung Montroyal. Die Zwingburg der Mosellande hat aber nicht lange gestanden; sie wurde nach dem Ryswicker Frieden von 1697 wieder geschleift. Unten am Abhang vor den steilen Weinbergen das alte Miniaturdorf Rießbach. In enger Schlucht schießt die Mosel dahin nach den beiden Orten Trarbach und Traben, die, zwar getrennt durch den Fluß, doch in sehr regem Verkehr mit einander stehen. Trarbach, eingeklemmt in ein Seitenthälchen und überragt von der malerischen Ruine Gräfinburg, auf der rechten — Traben, das etwas mehr Platz gefunden hat, weiter ausgedehnt auf der linken Seite. Beide Orte haben bedeutenden Weinbau, zusammen auf mehr als 700 Morgen, mit den hervorragenden Lagen Schloßberg, Ungsberg und Halsberg zu Trarbach, sowie Unterburg und Schimmelsberg zu Traben gehörig. Am Trarbacher Schloßberg wächst auch etwas guter Rothwein. Hier ist eine der merkwürdigsten Stätten des ganzen Moselgebietes, nicht blos des Weinbaues halber, sondern mehr noch wegen des ganz außerordentlich regen Weinhandels. In Trarbach-Traben hat besonders der Großhandel seinen Sitz, und es gehen viele tausend Fuder von diesem Hauptstapelplatz, der vornehmlich die Weine der Mittelmosel in seine riesigen Keller aufnimmt, alljährlich in alle Welt.

Im nebenbei gesagt durch seine vortrefflichen Weine bekannten Trarbacher Kasino wurde im Herbst 1845, als den

vom erſten deutſch-vlämiſchen Geſangfeſte zurückkehrenden Lieder-
tafeln von Koblenz und Trier ein Nachtfeſt gegeben wurde, und
als man den Mangel eines Moſelliedes lebhaft empfand, von
Dr. med. Graff aus Trarbach bei einem Trinkſpruche das
große Wort geſprochen: „Dem Manne, der ein Moſellied
ſchaffe, wie das von Claudius auf den Rhein »Am Rhein,
am Rhein, da wachſen unſere Reben«, dem Manne gebühre
ein Fuder des köſtlichſten Moſelweins". Das Trarbacher
Kaſino erwarb ſich im folgenden Frühjahr den unvergänglichen

Traben.

Ruhm, daß es ein Preisausſchreiben auf das beſte Volkslied
mit Melodie auf den Moſelwein erließ und als Preis ein
Fuder beſter Qualität ausſetzte. Für das Gold der Poeſie
das flüſſige Gold der Moſel! Welch eine Hochfluth von Liedern
ſich damals über das Moſelland ergoß, das kann man in dem
fröhlichen Büchlein von Dr. J. Blumberger „Moſelwein
und Moſellied" nachleſen. Es waren mehr als zweihundert
Lieder eingelaufen, aber es war viel Spreu unter dem Weizen,
und, da man den Fehler gemacht hatte, nur Muſiker als Preis-
richter zu ernennen, bekam den Preis, wie Blumberger ſagt,
„eine Hymne, von geſchickter, begeiſtert-ſchwungvoller Mache,
die aber weder nach Text noch nach Melodie auch nur im
entfernteſten geeignet war, Gemeingut des Volkes zu werden":

Sie ist heute vergessen! Aber es war auch eine Perle darunter, wenigstens im Text, das herrliche Mosellied von Theodor Reck: „Im weiten deutschen Lande zieht mancher Strom dahin", dessen Melodie einige Jahre später der Genius von Georg Schmitt schuf, sodaß es dann bald an der ganzen Mosel das Herz des Volkes eroberte. Und dennoch ist es nicht eigentlich das, was man haben wollte: „Ein Volkslied auf den Moselwein." Kann man ein solches überhaupt mit einem Preisausschreiben herbeizaubern? Muß es nicht wachsen, frei und ungezwungen, wie die wilden Rosen des Moselthales? — Es wird schon kommen!

Die Orte Trarbach und Traben haben das schwere Schicksal getheilt, durch Feuersbrunst arg verwüstet zu werden. Sie haben deswegen vorwiegend ein modernes Gepräge. Auf der Trabener Seite mündet die Nebenbahn, durch welche sie mit der großen Moseleisenbahn verbunden werden.

Gleich unterhalb Trabens das zugehörige Fischerdorf Litzig, und oben rechts auf der Höhe das Dorf Starken=

Kövenich bei Enkirch.

burg, von wo eine auf der Moselseite mit Reben be= deckte Berg= wand nach En= kirch zieht, dessen Häuser am Hange aufwärts klettern, und dessen Weingemarkung mit mehr als 500 Mor= gen eine der größten der Mosel ist. Gute Lagen: Stephansberg, Hinter= berg und Montaneubel. Von Enkirch stammte der Wein, den das Trarbacher Kasino bei der Liederkonkurrenz als Preis gab. Es war ein kostbares Fuder 1846er, Jungfernwein aus dem neuangelegten Batterieberge. Von dem gegenüber gelegenen malerischen Kövenich, Station der erwähnten Nebenbahn, prächtiger Blick auf die Enkircher Weinberge.

Cochem.

Altes Stadtthor in Cochem.

Mit Enkirch schließt die Reihe der Orte der Mittelmosel, in welchen die Hauptweine erzeugt werden. Der Weinbau bleibt im ganzen Thale freilich immer noch bedeutend, und in den steilen, oft in Terrassen angelegten Weinbergen wird ein Produkt erzielt, das zwar nicht den Anspruch auf die erste Reihe macht, das aber doch für sein Theil tüchtig beiträgt zum Ruhme der Moselweine. Das ist

gerade ein Vorzug der Moselproduktion, daß sie ihren rassigen
Wein nicht blos für große, sondern auch für bescheidene Geld=
beutel bietet. Es sind noch die Orte Burg, Reil, Pün=
derich, Briedel, Kaimt, Zell, Merl, Bullay,
Alf, Aldegund, Neef, Bremm, Eller, Ediger,
Nehren, Senheim, Senhals, Mesenich, Briedern,
Poltersdorf, Beilstein, Ellenz, Fankel, Bruttig,
Ernst, Valwig und Sehl zu nennen. Weinhandel wird
betrieben in Enkirch, Pünderich, Zell, Merl, Aldegund, Ediger,
Ellenz, Beilstein, und Bruttig.

Der Weinbau der Strecke von Piesport bis Cochem
umfaßt ca. 3200 ha = 12 800 Morgen, welche jährlich im
Durchschnitt etwa 9000 Fuder, d. h. mehr als die Hälfte
der ganzen Produktion an der Mittel= und Untermosel,
erzeugen.

Die Mosel von Cochem bis Coblenz.

Zwischen Cochem und Clotten macht die Mosel noch ein=
mal einen scharfen Bogen, um dann in sanfteren Windungen
den Schlußlauf bis Coblenz zu vollenden. Die steilen Ufer=
ränder schauen meistens rechts nach Nordwest und links
nach Südost. Nur in der Nähe von Cochem und dann
auf der kurzen Strecke
zwischen Cobern und
Winningen strömt
die Mosel so, daß
die Breitseite der
Weinberge dem Süden
zugekehrt ist. Die gün=
stigere Besonnung dieser La=
gen bewirkt, daß an der unteren
Mosel die drei Orte Cochem,

Burghaus Kurbisch und Castorkirche
in Carden.

Cobern und Winningen sich durch Erzeugung besserer Weine
ganz besonders hervorthun.

In den übrigen Orten werden in kunstvoll angelegten, vorzüglich gepflegten Terrassen-Weinbergen hauptsächlich mittlere Qualitäten produzirt, sämmtlich ausgezeichnet durch gute Gähre und echte Moselrasse. Staunend ruht der Blick auf den schmalen Rebenstreifen, die der Winzer mit unermüdlichem Fleiß und unverwüstlicher Ausdauer den oft nur schwer zugänglichen Klippen mit unsäglicher Mühe Stückchen um Stückchen abgetrotzt hat.

Hier ist die Strecke des Moselthales, in welcher die märchenhafte Romantik ihren Hauptglanz erreicht. In der engen Thalschlucht kleben die Orte an der Bergwand, die alten Häuser, Zeugen einer längst vergangenen Zeit, kreuz und quer durcheinander geschoben, überragt von malerischem Burggemäuer. Hier ist das sogenannte „Ritterthal" der Mosel, wo auf einer Strecke von etwa neun Stunden nicht weniger als zwölf Ritterburgen auf den Fluß hinunterschauen.

Cochem gilt als ein Glanzpunkt der Mosel. An der Moselkrümmung beim Dörfchen Sehl öffnet sich der Blick auf die berühmte Landschaft von Cochem, in welcher vor allem die über der Stadt auf steilen Felsen sich erhebende Reichsburg Cochem fesselt. Es ist ein herrliches Stimmungsbild, hoch oben das im echten mittelalterlichen Burgenstil — nicht in einem Phantasiestil — neu ausgebaute Schloß mit den zackigen Spitzdächern der vielen Thürme und Thürmchen, und dann unten am Felsen die alte Moselstadt, fast nicht minder eckig und kantig als das Schloß. Hinter der Stadt ragt aus dem wildromantischen Endertthal die Winneburg auf, und gegenüber am anderen Ufer der Mosel dehnt sich der Flecken Cond.

Der Weinbau bei Cochem und Cond umfaßt mehr als 400 Morgen und das Produkt aus einigen guten Lagen wird in der Neuzeit zu den besseren Moselweinen gezählt. In den beiden Orten blüht ein lebhafter Weinhandel. Bei Cochem beginnt der große Tunnel, der die Moselbahn aufwärts führt, mit 4,2 Kilometer Länge der bedeutendste Deutschlands. Von Cochem abwärts läuft die Bahn dicht am Flusse weiter fast bis Coblenz.

Ruine Bischofstein
bei Hatzenport.

In steilen, fel=
sigen, nur mühsam zu
bebauenden Lagen zieht
sich der Weinbau die Mosel hinunter nach Clotten
und Pommern, die zusammen zwischen 600 und 700
Morgen Weinberge haben. In Clotten wird auch Wein=
handel betrieben. Dann folgen Treis mit etwa 180
Morgen und schräg gegenüber Carden. Ernst und er=
haben ist der Charakter der Landschaft, aus welcher Carden
mit der alten Castorkirche und dem malerischen Burghause
weihevoll herausschaut. Zwischen Müden und Moselkern
rechts das enge Lützerthal, in dem bei Lütz noch Reben gebaut
werden, und links das wilde Elzthal mit der Burg Elz, der
vollständig erhaltenen Ritterburg aus dem Mittelalter. Alles
ist echt an ihr. Sie ist ein rechtes Wahrzeichen der Mosel.
Ueber Burgen geht es weiter nach Hatzenport, wo mitten
in Terrassen=Weinbergen die Ruinen der Burg Bischofstein den
Berghang gar prächtig schmücken. Hatzenport hat über 200
Morgen Weinberge mit der besseren Lage Tafelgutberg. Nun
kommen Brodenbach, Loef und Alken mit dem altersgrauen

Gemäuer der doppelthürmigen Feste Thurant, die im drei=
zehnten Jahrhundert einer Berennung so lange widerstand,
daß die belagernden Truppen 3000 Fuder Wein weggezecht
haben sollen. Ueber Katenes, Oberfell, Moselsürsch,
Lehmen, das durch Rothweinproduktion bekannt ist, Kühr,
Niederfell und Gondorf strömt die Mosel weiter nach
Cobern, Dieblich und Winningen, wo sich der Wein=
bau sowohl nach Menge als auch nach Güte noch einmal zu einer
hervorragenden Leistung aufschwingt. Cobern hat etwa 180
Morgen Weinberge und Winningen nicht weniger als ungefähr
620 Morgen; zu Dieblich gehören nur wenige Weinberge.
Berühmt ist die auf dem linken Ufer der Mosel an steiler
Felsenwand in zahlreichen Terrassen zwischen Cobern und
Winningen sich aufbauende und zu beiden Orten gehörige Lage
Uhlen. Bei Cobern werden noch besonders genannt die Lagen
Fahrberg und Rosenberg und bei Winningen, unterhalb der
Ortschaft, die Lage Röttchen, die bis obenhin mit Reben
bestockt ist. In Winningen wird auch Weinhandel betrieben.

Der alte fröhliche Brauch, die Weinlese mit einem Winzer=
feste zu beschließen, ist an der Mosel nach und nach verloren
gegangen. Nur in Winningen haben sich Ueberbleibsel davon
erhalten, jedoch feiern heutzutage das Winzerfest die jungen
Burschen im schwarzen Rock, auf dem Kopfe den Zylinder=
hut, und die Mädchen in weißen Kleidern. Das wäre also
die Poesie des Weinbaues in Gala. Aber beim Festmahle
wird nur von Zinngeschirr gespeist, und so kommt denn auch
die gute alte Zeit dabei zu ihrem Rechte.

Lay, Güls und Moselweiß sind die letzten Orte
der unteren Mosel, wo Reben sich im Flusse spiegeln. Groß
ist ihre Zahl daselbst nicht mehr. Die Poesie des Weinbaues
an der Mosel klingt aus mit der hübschen Legende vom
„Miseräbelchen", welche Simrock in seinen Rheinsagen nach
Güls verlegt. „Miseräbelchen" heißen bekanntlich die an der
Untermosel üblichen Schöppchen, und dieser Name wird ihnen
wohl in alle Ewigkeit hinein verbleiben.

Auf der Strecke Cochem bis Coblenz dienen ungefähr
925 Hektar = 3700 Morgen dem Weinbau und die jähr=
liche Durchschnittsernte mag etwa 2700 Fuder betragen, d. h.
etwas weniger als ein Fünftel der gesammten Weinernte an
der Mittel= und Untermosel.

Moselweinbau gibt es in unmittelbarer Nähe von
C o b l e n z nicht. Aber dennoch ist Coblenz am Ende des
Produktionsgebietes des Moselweines ebenso mit demselben
verwachsen wie Trier am Anfange, und wenn es auch heißt
„Coblenz am Rhein", so ist und bleibt
Coblenz doch auch eine echte Moselstadt.

Moselfähre bei Winningen.

Motiv aus Winningen.

Nach der Moselseite hat Coblenz
sein altes Gesicht aus dem
Mittelalter behalten, nach der
Rheinseite, wo sich die Stadt
später noch ausdehnte, nicht.
Ohne Zweifel hat auch das
Leben der Stadt in früheren Jahrhunderten an der Moselfront
am frischesten pulsirt. Die heute noch stehende im Jahre 1344
erbaute Moselbrücke verband Coblenz mit dem verkehrsreichen
Lützel=Coblenz, bis dieses nach anderem harten Schicksal 1688 bei
schwerer Kriegsnoth vollends über den Haufen geschossen wurde,
so daß der Rest der Gemeinde 14 Jahre später mit Neuendorf
vereinigt wurde. Die Brücke spielte ehemals bei seltsamen Ge=
bräuchen eine Rolle. Auf ihr verzehrte der hochwohlweise
Magistrat am Neujahrstage ein niederländisches Käschen, ein
Kapaunenpaar, einen Kuchen und ein Viertel gesottener Eier;
am Walpurgisabend spazierten die beiden Bürgermeister auf ihr

hin und her, dabei die ihnen begegnenden Frauen und Jung=
frauen mit Blumen beschenkend; und am Prediger=Kirchweih=
feste durfte das junge Volk auf ihr tanzen, bis die Nacht
hereinbrach. An der Brücke, der alten Burg gegenüber, stellten
sich am Namenstage des Erzbischofs Edelbürger in Helm und
Harnisch auf, um einen Ehrentrunk von drei Fuder Wein in
Empfang zu nehmen.

Die noch jetzt gut erhaltene erzbischöfliche Burg an
der Moselbrücke wurde 1276 er=
baut, wobei es nicht ohne
Krakehl mit den Coblenzer Bür=
gern abging, die solch ein
festes Ding innerhalb der Stadt=
mauern eigentlich gar nicht dul=

Schöffenhaus in Coblenz.

Alte Burg
in Coblenz
und Moselbrücke.

den wollten. Die Kurfürsten wohnten vorübergehend oft in
der Burg. Dabei mag mancher volle Henkelkrug guten
Moselweines den Weg allen Weines gewandert sein! In der
Franzosenzeit ging die alte Burgenherrlichkeit zu Ende. Die
Burg wurde verkauft und zu einer Fabrik lackirter Blech=
waaren degradirt. Diesem Zustande hat die Stadt Coblenz
im Jahre 1896 ein Ende gemacht. Sie hat den alterthüm=
lichen, merkwürdigen Bau angekauft, wird ihn würdig be=
nutzen und erhalten.

Coblenz hat sehr bedeutenden Weinhandel, und daß dabei
der Moselwein die Hauptrolle spielt, hat für denjenigen, der
weiß, mit welch feinem Verständniß man daselbst das rassige
Produkt der Mosel aufnimmt, nichts Ueberraschendes. Der
Weinhandel von Coblenz ist stolz auf seine Moselweine.

Bei Coblenz entführt der Rhein die Mosel in die weite,
weite Welt. Ihren Fluthen ist es nicht beschieden, daheim
zu bleiben, und so oft sie sich auch erneuern, sie müssen ewig
wandern, fortwandern aus der Heimath. Nicht anders ist es
mit ihren Weinen. So oft auch die Sonnenstrahlen an den
Schieferwänden die Traube reifen, der Wein muß hinaus in
die weite, weite Welt. Es gibt nur e i n e n Moselwein. Wo
sollen sich die durstigen Menschenkinder den Moselwein anders
holen als an der Mosel!

Inhaltsverzeichniß.

Bilderverzeichniß.

*) Nach Photographien der Originale. — Die übrigen Bilder sind von Professor Anton Lewy gezeichnet.

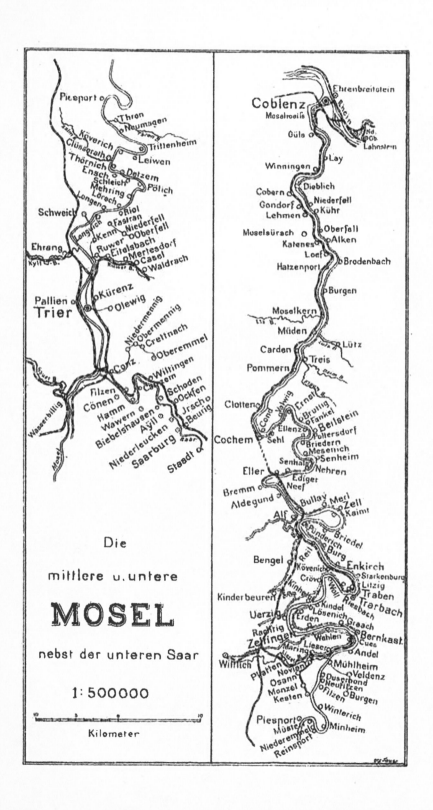

Die

mittlere u. untere

MOSEL

nebst der unteren Saar

1 : 500000

Kilometer

Moselweinlied

von

Karl Heinrich Koch.

In Musik gesetzt von

Carl Wegeler.

Moselweinlied.

Frisch mit Humor.

Gesang.

Pianoforte.

1. Nun putzt die Glä = ser
2. Er ist nicht voll und
3. So freu = dig wie die
4. Und fröh = lich baut im
5. So plagt uns gar kein

1. bli = tze = blank, es kommt der rech = te Tropfen, und
2. dick und schwer und auch nicht plump und stuf = tig; er
3. Sonne strahlt ins Mo = sel = thal her = nie = der, und
4. Sonnen = brand der Win = zer sei = ne Re = ben, weil
5. Her = ze = leid, wir müs = sen wei = ter trin = ken, und

4

à tempo.
rit.

1. un = ter lau = tem Sang und Klang ziehn wir den er = sten
2. hat die al = ler = fein = ste Gähr, ist wie ein Rös = lein
3. wenn man sonst auch noch so prahlt, das gibt's ja gar nicht
4. lu = stig wird des Ze = chers Hand das Mo = sel = glas er =
2. soll = ten wir vor Se = lig = keit uns in die Ar = me

1. Sto = pfen.
2. duf = tig.
3. wie = der.
4. ho = ben.
5. sin = ken.

Der Wein ist deutsch, der

ritard.

1–5. Wein ift gut, ift ech = tes Mo = fel=

ritard.

a Tempo.

1–5. re = ben = blut, der Wein ift deutſch, der

a Tempo.

ad libitum!

1–5. Wein ift gut, ift ech = tes Mo = fel=

1—5. 'Re ⁎ ben ⁎ blut.　　　　Schluß.

f

ff　　　　Fine.

CPSIA information can be obtained
at www.ICGtesting.com
Printed in the USA
BVHW022329120422
634083BV00016B/746